a gallic trio

charles munch
paul paray
pierre monteux

discographies
compiled by
john hunt

acknowledgement

these publications have been made possible by contributions or advance subscriptions from the following

Richard Ames
Stathis Arfanis
J.M. Blyth*
Edward Chibas*
Robert Dandois
Richard Dennis
Ronald Easdon
Henry Fogel*
Peter Fülop
Jean-Pierre Goossens
Alan Haine
Tadashi Hasegawa*
Bodo Igesz
Andrew Keener
Koji Kinoshita
Elisabeth Legge-Schwarzkopf*
John Mallinson*
Carlo Marinelli
Bruce Morrison
Alan Newcombe
Jim Parsons*
David Patmore*
James Pearson
Patrick Russell
Tom Scragg*
Robert Simmons
Michael Tanner
Nigel Wood*
Stephen Wright

Stefano Angeloni
Yoshihiro Asada
Brian Capon
George Cobby
Dennis Davis
John Derry
Hans-Peter Ebner*
Nobuo Fukumoto
Philip Goodman
Johann Gratz
Michael Harris*
Naoya Hirabayashi
E.M. Johnson
Rodney Kempster
Detlef Kissmann
Douglas MacIntosh
Neil Mantle
Philip Moores
W. Moyle
Hugh Palmer*
Laurence Pateman
J.A. Payne
Tully Potter
Ingo Schwarz
John Shackleton
Yoshihiko Suzuki*
Urs Weber*
Graeme Wright*
Ken Wyman

*indicates life subscriber

contents

- 7   introduction
- 9   charles munch
- 93   paul paray
- 147   pierre monteux

A Gallic Trio
Published by John Hunt.
Cover design by Richard Chluparty
© 2003 John Hunt
reprinted 2009
ISBN 978-1-901395-15-0

Sole distributors:
Travis & Emery,
17 Cecil Court,
London, WC2N 4EZ,
United Kingdom.
(+44) 20 7 459 2129.
sales@travis-and-emery.com

A gallic trio: an introduction

Nowadays it is probably politically incorrect to suggest that only a French-born musician can fully do justice to French music. The list of such specialists in the conducting field during the last century is extensive (names like Albert Wolff, Roger Desormiere, Gabriel Pierné and Desiré-Emile Inghelbrecht spring to mind), but surprisingly short in internationally well-known names until we reach World War II and after. From the later 1940s onwards the burgeoning record industry in the USA encouraged the employment of stars who would also ensure success at the concert box office, and it was thus that some eminent French names were invited to contract themselves to major American labels.

Lesser-known French repertoire was therefore exposed to a wider listening public, although the mainstay of the catalogues was still what we would now describe as standard classical fare. The Wagner recordings which our three conductors made possess perhaps greater transparency than what we would expect from Reiner, Szell or Stokowski; their Brahms is surprisingly mainstream, their Beethoven may be a little more variable. You will find no Mahler or Bruckner symphonies, however (I hear sighs of relief from certain quarters).

My usual format is followed for these discographies: main issues for most territories except Japan, in all the main categories of 78, 45, LP, CD, VHS, DVD Audio and DVD Video. Recording dates aim to be as precise as possible, and a central column lists orchestras, choirs, participating vocal soloists and instrumentalists (I am, as always, glad to hear from collectors who can add to or correct existing data).

Special thanks for help with these particular discographies goes to Richard Ames, Richard Chlupaty, Syd Gray, John Hancock, Bill Holland and Roderick Krüsemann.

John Hunt   Copyright 2003

Royal Festival Hall
(General Manager: John Denison, C.B.E.)
Thursday, December 9, 1965, at 8

ELGAR   Introduction and Allegro for Strings

RAVEL   Daphnis et Chloë, Suite No. 2

BRAHMS   Symphony No. 1 in C minor

MUNCH   New Philharmonia Orchestra

Leader: Hugh Bean

charles munch
1891-1968

ISAAC ALBENIZ (1860-1909)

ibéria, piano suite arranged for orchestra by arbos
paris	orchestre	lp: concert hall SMSA 2494
november-december 1966	national	lp: musidisc FC 437

LOUIS AUBERT (1877-1968)

habanera pour orchestre
paris	conservatoire	78: hmv (france) DB 11109
28 april 1944	orchestra	cd: classical record ACR 40-41

la nuit ensorselée, ballet suite based on themes of chopin
paris	conservatoire	78: hmv (france) DB 11100-11102
15 april 1944	orchestra	cd: classical record ACR 40-41
		recording completed on 28 april 1944

ALFRED BACHELET (1864-1944)

un jardin
paris	conservatoire	78: action artistique AA 8
january 1943	orchestra	

JOHANN SEBASTIAN BACH (1685-1750)

brandenburg concerto no 1
tanglewood   boston   lp: victor LM 2182/LM 6140/LSC 6140
8 july   symphony   lp: rca camden classics CCV 5007
1957   cd: victor (japan) BVCC 7901

brandenburg concerto no 2
tanglewood   boston   lp: victor LM 2182/LM 6140/LSC 6140
9 july   symphony   lp: rca camden classics CCV 5007
1957   cd: victor (japan) BVCC 7901

brandenburg concerto no 3
tanglewood   boston   lp: victor LM 2182/LM 6140/LSC 6140
8 july   symphony   lp: rca camden classics CCV 5007
1957   cd: victor (japan) BVCC 7901

bach **brandenburg concerto no 4**
tanglewood   boston   lp: victor LM 2198/LM 6140/LSC 6140
8 july   symphony   lp: rca camden classics CCV 5033
1957   cd: victor (japan) BVCC 7902

brandenburg concerto no 5
tanglewood   boston   lp: victor LM 2198/LM 6140/LSC 6140
9 july   symphony   lp: rca camden classics CCV 5033
1957   cd: victor (japan) BVCC 7902

brandenburg concerto no 6
tanglewood   boston   lp: victor LM 2198/LM 6140/LSC 6140
9 july   symphony   lp: rca camden classics CCV 5033
1957   cd: victor (japan) BVCC 7902

violin concerto in a minor bwv 1041
boston   boston   lp: victor VIC 1033/VICS 1033
26 december   symphony
1960   laredo, violin

cantata no 189 "meine seele rühmt und preist"
paris   conservatoire   78: hmv (france) DB 5193-5194
22 december   orchestra   cd: classical record ACR 43-44
1942   bernac

SAMUEL BARBER (1910-1981)

adagio for strings
boston   boston   lp: victor LM 2105/LSC 2105/RB 16025
1 april   symphony   cd: rca/bmg 09026 614242
1957

meditation and dance of vengeance/medea
boston   boston   lp: victor LM 2917/LSC 2917/VIC 1391/
10 april   symphony   VICS 1391
1957   cd: rca/bmg 09026 614242

HENRY BARRAUD born 1900

symphony no 3
paris   orchestre   lp: véga C30 A351
10 december   national   cd: accord 461 745
1961

BEETHOVEN
Symphonie N° 6 "PASTORALE"

CHARLES MÜNCH
ROTTERDAMS PHILHARMONISCH ORKEST

LUDWIG VAN BEETHOVEN (1770-1827)

symphony no 1
boston	boston	45: victor WDM 1622
27 december	symphony	lp: victor LM 1200
1950		cd: rca/bmg 09026 613992

symphony no 3 "eroica"
boston	boston	lp: victor LM 2233
2 december	symphony	cd: rca/bmg 09026 613992
1957		

symphony no 4
stockholm	orchestre	cd: disques montaigne MUN 2061
25 august	national	cd: valois V 4825
1964		

symphony no 5
boston	boston	lp: victor LM 1923/VIC 1035/
2 may	symphony	VICS 1035
1955		cd: rca/bmg GD 68032/09026 615512

symphony no 6 "pastoral"
tanglewood	boston	lp: victor LM 1997/RB 16006/
16 august	symphony	AGL1-2442
1955		cd: victor (japan) BVCC 7094

rotterdam	rotterdam	lp: concert hall SMSA 2527
september	philharmonic	cd: valois V 4829
1966		cd: scribendum SC 012

symphony no 7
boston	boston	78: victor M 1360
19 december	symphony	45: victor WDM 1360
1949		lp: victor LM 1034
		lp: hmv (france) FALP 106

beethoven **symphony no 8**
london 2 october 1947	conservatoire orchestra	78: decca K 1933-1935 lp: decca LX 3053 lp: london (usa) LPS 111 cd: polygram (japan) POCL 4602
boston 30 november 1958	boston symphony	lp: victor LM 6066/LSC 6066

symphony no 9 "choral"

boston
21-22
december
1958
	boston
	symphony
	new england
	conservatory
	chorus
	l.price
	forrester
	polieri
	tozzi
		lp: victor LM 6066/LSC 6066/VIC 1114/
		    VICS 1114/VICS 1660/VICS 6003/
		    AGL1-3007/26.41172/26.48071/
		    GL 42085/GL 43700
		lp: rca camden classics CCV 5021
		cd: emi CZS 575 4772

tokyo 27 december 1962	tokyo philharmonic orchestra and chorus nikikai chorus gamon ono mori okamura	cd: kapelle (japan) 32GD 174 947

beethoven **piano concerto no 1**

boston	boston	cd: as-disc AS 335-336
1 november	symphony	
1960	richter, piano	

boston	boston	lp: victor LM 2544/LM 6097/LSC 2544/
2-3	symphony	LSC 6097/RB 16280/SB 2149/
november	richter, piano	VICS 1478
1960		lp: melodiya D 010025-010026
		cd: rca/bmg GD 86804

piano concerto no 3

boston	boston	lp: discocorp RR 553
1-3	symphony	lp: columbia (japan) OS 7116
november	haskil, piano	cd: music and arts CD 716/CD 1096
1956		

piano concerto no 5 "emperor"

paris	conservatoire	78: columbia (france) LFX 679-683
11 june	orchestra	lp: columbia (france) 33FHX 5006
1944	m.long, piano	lp: toshiba GR 2194
		cd: classical record ACR 43-44
		cd: dante LYS 510

violin concerto

boston	boston	lp: victor LM 1992/LSC 1992/RB 16124/
27-28	symphony	SB 2047
november	heifetz, violin	lp: hmv ALP 1437
1955		cd: rca/bmg RCD 15402/09026 617422/
		09026 617792/09026 689802

minuet in e flat ww0 3

boston	boston	45: victor WDM 1360
20 december	symphony	
1949		

beethoven **coriolan overture**
boston	boston	lp: victor LM 2015/LSC 2015/VICS 1471
26-27 february 1956	symphony	lp: rca camden classics CCV 5009

fidelio overture
boston	boston	lp: victor LM 2015/LSC 2015/VICS 1471
26-27 february 1956	symphony	lp: rca camden classics CCV 5009

die geschöpfe des prometheus, overture, adagio and finale
boston	boston	lp: victor LM 2522/LSC 2522
6 march	symphony	*overture only*
1960		lp: rca camden classics CCV 5009

leonore no 1 overture
boston	boston	lp: victor LM 2015/LSC 2015/VICS 1471
26 february 1956	symphony	lp: rca camden classics CCV 5009

leonore no 2 overture
boston	boston	lp: victor LM 2015/LSC 2015/VICS 1471
26 february	symphony	lp: rca camden classics CCV 5009
1956		cd: rca/bmg RD 68032

leonore no 3 overture
boston	boston	lp: victor LM 2015/LSC 2015/VICS 1471
27 february	symphony	lp: rca camden classics CCV 5009
1956		cd: rca/bmg RD 68032/09026 615512

die weihe des hauses overture
paris	orchestre	cd: disques montaigne MUN 2061
20 december 1963	national	cd: valois V 4825

HECTOR BERLIOZ (1803-1869)

symphonie fantastique

paris december 1948	orchestre national	78: columbia (france) LFX 880-885 78: columbia (italy) GQX 11349-11354 lp: emi trianon (france) TRX 6104 cd: classical record ACR 40-41
boston 14-15 november 1954	boston symphony	lp: victor LM 1900 lp: victor (italy) A12R 0179 lp: hmv ALP 1384 cd: rca/bmg 09026 684442/09026 614002

boston
9 april
1962
	boston
	symphony
		lp: victor LM 2608/LSC 2608/RB 6521/
		    SB 6521
		cd: rca/bmg RD 67202/RD 77352/
		    RD 87735/74321 341682

cambridge mass. 17 april 1962	boston symphony	vhs video: warner 4509 957103 dvd video: warner 0927 426682 *fourth and fifth movements only*
lisbon 23 june 1963	orchestre national	cd: disques montaigne MUN 2011 cd: valois V 4826
montreal 19 december 1963	cbc orchestra	cd: vai audio VAI 69427
budapest 15 april 1966	hungarian state orchestra	lp: hungaroton SLPX 11842 cd: philips 426 1032

paris
23-26
october
1967
	orchestre
	de paris
		lp: emi ASD 2342/CVL 2037/SME 91685/
		    1C063 10595/2C069 10595/
		    3C065 10595
		lp: angel 36517
		cd: emi CDC 747 3722/CDM 769 9572

world's encyclopaedia of recorded music second supplement (sidgwick and jackson 1953) mentions a columbia 78rpm version of the symphony conducted by munch with the conservatoire orchestra, however no other reference can be found to this recording

berlioz **harold en italie**

boston	boston	lp: victor LM 2228/LSC 2228/RB 16084/
31 march	symphony	SB 2016/GL 42718
1958	primrose, viola	cd: rca/bmg 09026 652822/09026 684442

roméo et juliette

boston	boston	45: victor WDM 6011
22-23	symphony	lp: victor LM 6011
february	harvard glee	lp: victor (italy) B12R 0111-0112
1953	and radcliffe	lp: hmv ALP 1179-1180
	choirs	lp: hmv (france) FALP 271-272
	roggero	cd: rca/bmg GD 60681/09026 606812
	chabay	*excerpts*
	sze	lp: victor LM 6028

boston	boston	lp: victor LD 6098/LDS 6098
23-24	symphony	cd: rca/bmg 74321 341682
april	new england	
1961	conservatory	
	chorus	
	elias	
	valletti	
	tozzi	

berlioz **la reine mab/roméo et juliette**

paris	conservatoire	78: decca X 281
30 may	orchestra	78: london (usa) LA 208
1949		lp: decca LXT 2512
		lp: london (usa) LLP 3
		cd: decca 433 4052

roméo seul; fete chez capulet; scene d'amour/roméo et juliette

paris	conservatoire	78: decca X 293-295
1 june	orchestra	78: london (usa) LA 208
1949		lp: decca LXT 2512
		lp: london (usa) LLP 3
		cd: decca 433 4052

chasse royal et orage/les troyens

paris	conservatoire	78: decca X 301
30 may	orchestra	78: london (usa) T 5678
1949		lp: decca LXT 2512
		lp: london (usa) LLP 3
		cd: decca 433 4052

boston	boston	lp: victor LM 2438/LSC 2438/RB 16254/
6 april	symphony	SB 2125
1959		cd: rca/bmg 09026 684442/09026 614002

boston	boston	cd: boston symphony orchestra BSOCD 4
26 january	symphony	
1963		

chicago	chicago	vhs video: video artists international
27 february	symphony	VAI 69605
1963		dvd video: video artists international
		VAIDVD 4226

berlioz **la damnation de faust**

boston	boston	lp: victor LM 6114
21-22	symphony	lp: victor (france) A 630210-630212
february	new england	lp: victor (italy) C12R 0133-0135
1954	conservatory	lp: hmv ALP 1225-1227
	chorus	cd: rca/bmg 09026 684442
	danco	*excerpts*
	poleri	45: victor ERA 250
	singher	lp: victor SP 33-181
	gramm	
	boatwright	

menuet des follets; ballet des sylphes; marche hongroise/la damnation de faust

philadelphia	philadelphia	lp: columbia (usa) ML 5923/MS 6523
13 march	orchestra	cd: sony SBK 53255
1963		

l'enfance du christ

boston	boston	lp: victor LM 6053/VIC 6006/VICS 6006
23-24	symphony	cd: rca/bmg 09026 684442/09026 612342
december	new england	
1956	conservatory	
	chorus	
	kopleff	
	valletti	
	souzay	
	tozzi	

berlioz **les nuits d'été, song cycle**

boston	boston	lp: victor LM 1907
12 april	symphony	cd: rca/bmg 09026 684442/09026 606812/
1955	de los angeles	GD 60681
		cd: testament SBT 3203

grande messe des morts

boston	boston	lp: victor LM 6077/LDS 6077
26-27	symphony	RB 16224-16225/SB 2096-2097
april	new england	cd: rca/bmg 09026 694442/09026 606812
1959	conservatory	
	chorus	
	simoneau	

munich	bavarian	lp: dg SLPEM 139 264-139 265/
6-8	radio orchestra	2707 032/2726 050
july	and chorus	cd: dg 439 7052
1967	schreier	

béatrice et bénédict, overture

boston	boston	78: victor 12-3078
20 december	symphony	78: hmv DB 4321
1949		45: victor WDM 1700/ERA 68
		45: hmv (france) 7RF 124
		lp: victor LM 1700
		lp: hmv ALP 1245

boston	boston	lp: victor LM 2438/LSC 2438/RB 16254/
1 december	symphony	SB 2125
1958		cd: rca/bmg 09026 684442/09026 617212/
		09026 614002/74321 212832

berlioz **benvenuto cellini, overture**

walthamstow 11 october 1946	paris conservatoire orchestra	lp: decca LXT 2677/LW 5014 lp: london (usa) LLP 466/LD 9019 cd: decca 433 4052
boston 6 april 1959	boston symphony	lp: victor LM 2438/LSC 2438/RB 16254/ SB 2125 cd: rca/bmg 09026 684442/09026 614002
besancon 13 september 1966	orchestre national	cd: disques montaigne MUN 2011 cd: valois V 4826

le carnaval romain, overture

boston 1 december 1958	boston symphony	lp: victor LM 2438/LSC 2438/RB 16254/ SB 2125 cd: rca/bmg 09026 684442/09026 614002/ 09026 617212/74321 212832

le corsaire, overture

paris 27 may 1948	conservatoire orchestra	78: decca K 1948 lp: decca LXT 2677/LW 5014 lp: london (usa) LLP 466/LD 9019 cd: decca 433 4052 cd: emi CZS 575 4772
boston 1 december 1958	boston symphony	lp: victor LM 2438/LSC 2438/RB 16254/ SB 2125 cd: rca/bmg 09026 684442/09026 617212/ 09026 614002/74321 212832
montreal 25 september 1967	orchestre national	cd: disques montaigne MUN 2011 cd: valois V 4826

GEORGES BIZET (1838-1875)

symphony in c

london 2-6 june 1947	london philharmonic	78: decca K 1781-1784 78: london (usa) LA 194 lp: london (usa) LPS 118
walthamstow 9-10 april 1963	royal philharmonic	lp: readers digest RD 47/RDS 47 cd: chesky CD 7
boston 1-4 february 1964	boston symphony	cd: boston symphony orchestra BSOCD 4
paris 10-11 november 1966	orchestre national	lp: concert hall SMSA 2495 cd: ades 13.2242 cd: emi CZS 575 4772 cd: scribendum SC 012

patrie, overture

paris 10-11 november 1966	orchestre national	lp: concert hall SMSA 2495 cd: ades 13.2242 cd: scribendum SC 012

bizet **l'arlésienne, suite**
london	new	lp: decca PFS 4127
4-5	philharmonia	lp: london (usa) SPC 21023
january		cd: decca 444 0332
1967		

carmen, suite
london	new	lp: decca PFS 4127
4-5	philharmonia	lp: london (usa) SPC 21023
january		cd: decca 444 0332
1967		

jeux d'enfants, suite
paris	orchestre	lp: concert hall SMSA 2495
10-11	national	cd: ades 13.2242
november		cd: scribendum SC 012
1966		

danse bohémienne/la jolie fille de perth
london	london	78: decca K 1784
5 june	philharmonic	78: london (usa) LA 194
1947		

EASLEY BLACKWOOD (born 1933)

symphony no 1
boston	boston	lp: victor LM 2352/LSC 2352
9 november	symphony	cd: cédille 90000 016
1959		

ERNEST BLOCH (1880-1959)

violin concerto in a minor
paris   conservatoire   78: columbia LX 819-822
22-23   orchestra   78: columbia (australia) LOX 455-458
march   szigeti, violin   78: columbia (usa) M 380
1939   lp: columbia (usa) ML 4679
                                             lp: discocorp WSA 701
                                             cd: pearl GEMMCD 9938
                                             cd: symposium SYM 1226

schelomo, for cello and orchestra
boston   boston   lp: victor LM 2109/LSC 2109/RB 16027
30 january   symphony
1957   piatigorsky, cello

concerto grosso no 1
new york   new york   cd: new york philharmonic NYPCD 9906
8 february   philharmonic
1948

ALEXANDER BORODIN (1833-1887)

in the steppes of central asia
paris   orchestre   lp: concert hall SMSA 2511
october-   national   lp: musidisc FC 439
november   cd: scribendum SC 012
1966

JOHANNES BRAHMS (1833-1897)

symphony no 1

boston 19 november 1956	boston symphony	lp: victor LM 2097/LM 6902/LSC 2097/ LSC 6902/26.48072/VIC 1062/ VICS 1062 cd: rca/bmg 09026 607882
paris 1 january 1968	orchestre de paris	lp: emi 1C063 10596/2C069 10596/ 3C065 10596 cd: emi CMS 769 9572 *recording completed on 12 january 1968*

symphony no 2

boston 5 december 1955	boston symphony	lp: victor LM 1959/AGL1-2702 cd: rca/bmg 09026 606822
prague 11 september 1956	boston symphony	cd: multisonic 310 0252
chartres 16 november 1965	orchestre national	cd: disques montaigne MUN 2021 cd: valois V 4827

brahms **symphony no 4**
boston	boston	78: victor M 1399
10-11	symphony	45: victor WDM 1399
april		lp: victor LM 1086
1950		lp: hmv (france) FALP 144
		lp: hmv (italy) QALP 144
		lp: rca camden classics CCV 5032
boston	boston	lp: victor LM 2297/LM 6902/LSC 2297/
27 october	symphony	LSC 6902/RB 16177/SB 2060
1958		cd: rca/bmg 09026 612062

piano concerto no 1
boston	boston	lp: victor LM 2274/LSC 2274/RB 16217/
9 april	symphony	SB 2047
1958	graffman, piano	

piano concerto no 2
boston	boston	45: victor WDM 1728
11 august	symphony	lp: victor LM 1728
1952	rubinstein,	lp: victor (italy) A12R 0041
	piano	lp: hmv ALP 1123
		lp: hmv (france) FALP 250
		cd: rca/bmg 09026 630112/09026 630 002/
		09026 630 222
boston	boston	cd: as-disc AS 335-336
1 november	symphony	
1960	richter, piano	

brahms **violin concerto**
amsterdam	concertgebouw	78: decca AK 2055-2059
13-14	orchestra	78: london (usa) LA 87
september	renardy, violin	lp: decca LXT 2566
1948		lp: london (usa) LLP 1
		cd: dante LYS 478
		cd: dutton CDEA 5024
		dutton gives recording date as 27 june 1948

haydn variations
tokyo	tokyo	cd: japan P23 G541
25 december	philharmonic	
1962		

tragic overture
boston	boston	lp: victor LM 1959/AGL1-2702
5 december	symphony	
1955		

MAX BRUCH (1838-1920)

violin concerto no 1
boston	boston	78: hmv DB 21415-21417
18 january	symphony	45: victor WDM 1547
1951	menuhin, violin	lp: victor LM 122/LM 1797
		lp: hmv (france) FBLP 1016

EMANUEL CHABRIER (1841-1894)

bourrée fantasque
new york	new york	cd: dante LYS 543
19 december	philharmonic	
1948		

ERNEST CHAUSSON (1855-1899)

symphony in b flat
boston	boston	lp: victor LM 2647/LSC 2647/RB 6528/
26 february	symphony	SB 6528
1962		cd: rca/bmg GD 60683/09026 606832/
		74321 845912

poeme pour violon et orchestre
new york	new york	lp: discocorp RR 550
2 january	philharmonic	cd: music and arts CD 550/CD 837
1949	neveu, violin	cd: dante LYS 389-390
boston	boston	lp: victor LM 1988/RB 16166/
14 december	symphony	VIC 1058/VICS 1058
1955	oistrakh, violin	cd: rca/bmg GD 60683/09026 606832/
		74321 845912

FREDERIC CHOPIN (1810-1849)

piano concerto no 1

boston	boston	lp: victor LM 2468/LSC 2468/VIC 1030/
14 march	symphony	VICS 1030
1960	graffman, piano	

piano concerto no 2

boston	boston	45: victor ERB 51
29 november	symphony	lp: victor LM 1871
1954	brailowsky,	lp: victor (france) A 630242
	piano	lp: hmv ALP 1321
		cd: rca/bmg 09026 616562

GEORGES DANDELOT (1895-1976)

symphony in d

paris	conservatoire	78: action artisrique AA 30
june	orchestra	
1943		

CLAUDE DEBUSSY (1862-1918)

la mer

paris 2 march 1942	conservatoire orchestra	78: hmv (france) W 1500-1502 cd: classical record ACR 40-41 cd: dante LYS 357

boston
9-10
december
1956
	boston
	symphony
		lp: victor LM 2111/LSC 2111/VIC 1041/
		    VICS 1041
		cd: rca/bmg GD 86719/09026 615002/
		    74321 845912/74321 212932

cambridge mass. 17 april 1962	boston symphony	vhs video: teldec 4509 957103 dvd video: teldec 0927 426682 *jeux de vagues only from this televised performance*
paris 8 may 1962	orchestre national	cd: disques montaigne TCE 8730 cd: valois V 4828 cd: living stage LS 1042
paris february 1968	orchestre national	lp: concert hall SMSA 2579 lp: musidisc FC 408 cd: accord 22.0272 cd: scribendum SC 012

fantaisie pour piano et orchestre

paris 8 may 1962	orchestre national henriot- schweitzer, piano	cd: disques montaigne TCE 8730 cd: valois V 4828
strassburg 13 june 1962	orchestre national henriot- schweitzer, piano	cd: ina EURM 2009

debussy **prélude a l'apres-midi d'un faune**
boston	boston	victor unpublished
26 february	symphony	
1956		

boston	boston	lp: victor LM 1984/LSC 1984
14 march	symphony	
1956		

boston	boston	lp: victor LM 2668/LSC 2668/RB 6540/
13 march	symphony	SB 6540
1962		cd: rca/bmg GD 86719/74321 845912/
		74321 212932

paris	orchestre	lp: concert hall SMSA 2761
february	national	cd: scribendum SC 012
1968		

trois nocturnes
paris	orchestre	lp: concert hall SMSA 2579
february	national	lp: musidisc FC 408
1968		cd: accord 22.0272

nuages et fetes/trois nocturnes
boston	boston	lp: victor LM 2668/LSC 2668/RB 6540/
13 march	symphony	SB 6540
1962		cd: rca/bmg RD 67192/74321 845912

debussy **images pour orchestre**

boston	boston	lp: victor LM 2282/LSC 2282/VIC 1162/ VICS 1162
16 december	symphony	
1957		cd: rca/bmg 09026 619562
		gigues only
		cd: rca/bmg 74321 845912

ibéria/images pour orchestre

london	paris	78: decca K 1763-1765
30 september-	conservatoire	45: london (usa) EDA 51
1 october	orchestra	cd: dante LYS 438
1947		
paris	orchestre	cd: disques montaigne TCE 8730
8 may	national	cd: valois V 4828
1962		cd: living stage LS 1042
paris	orchestre	lp: concert hall SMSA 2761
october-	national	lp: musidisc FC 437
november		cd: scribendum SC 012
1966		

printemps, suite symphonique

boston	boston	lp: victor LM 2668/LSC 2668/RB 6540/ SB 6540
13 march	symphony	
1962		cd: rca/bmg GD 86719/74321 845912/ 74321 212932

debussy **berceuse héroique**
london	paris	78: decca K 1765/AX 490
1-2	conservatoire	45: london (usa) EDA 51
october	orchestra	
1947		

le martyre de saint sébastien
boston	boston	lp: victor LM 2030/VICS 1404
29-30	sym,phony	cd: rca/bmg 09026 614982
december	new england	
1957	conservatory	
	chorus	
	curtin	

la demoiselle élue
boston	boston	lp: victor LM 1907
11 april	symphony	cd: rca/bmg RD 79402
1955	de los angeles	cd: testament SBT 3203

MARCEL DELANNOY (1898-1962)

sérénade concertante pour violon et orchestre
paris	conservatoire	78: hmv (france) DB 5184-5186
21 july	orchestra	cd: classical record ACR 43-44
1941	merckel, violin	cd: dante LYS 357

danse des négrillons; apothéose/le pantoufle de vair
paris	conservatoire	78: hmv (france) DB 5186
21 july	orchestra	cd: classical record ACR 43-44
1941	merckel, violin	

PAUL DUKAS (1865-1935)

l'apprenti sorcier
boston	boston	lp: victor LM 2292/LSC 2292/RB 16155/
4 november	symphony	SB 2041
1957		cd: rca/bmg 09026 614002

HENRI DUTILLEUX (born 1916)

symphony no 2 "le double"
paris	orchestre	cd: disques montaigne TCE 8730
5 june	national	
1962		

paris	lamoureux	lp: erato STU 70278
april	orchestra	cd: erato 3984 223252
1965		

métaboles pour orchestre
paris	orchestre	lp: erato STU 70400
june	national	cd: erato 2292 456892
1967		

ANTONIN DVORAK (1841-1904)

symphony no 8
boston	boston	lp: victor LM 2629/LSC 2629/RB 6509/
13 march	symphony	SB 6509
1961		cd: rca/bmg 74321 740142

cello concerto
boston	boston	lp: victor LM 2490/LSC 2490/RB 16245/
7 march	symphony	SB 2114
1960	piatigorsky, cello	cd: rca/bmg 09026 614982

EDWARD ELGAR (1857-1934)

introduction and allegro for strings
boston	boston	lp: victor LM 2105/LSC 2105/RB 16025
3 april	symphony	cd: rca/bmg 09026 614242/74321 242172
1957		

GABRIEL FAURE (1845-1924)

ballade pour piano et orchestre
boston 2 april 1960	boston symphony henriot- schweitzer, piano	cd: music and arts CD 236

pavane
walthamstow 9 october 1946	paris conservatoire orchestre	78: decca K 1644 45: london (usa) EDA 37

pénélope, overture
boston 12 december 1959	boston symphony	cd: music and arts CD 236

pelléas et mélisande, suite
london 5 june 1947	london philharmonic	78: decca K 1740-1741 45: london (usa) EDA 58
boston 7 march 1959	boston symphony	cd: music and arts CD 236
philadelphia 14 march 1963	philadelphia orchestra	lp: columbia (usa) ML 5923/MS 6523 cd: sony SBK MFK 45543
tokyo 22 october 1966	orchestre national	cd: disques montaigne MUN 2031 cd: valois V 4829
boston 3 december 1966	boston symphony	cd: boston symphony orchestra BSOCD 4

PIERRE-OCTAVE FERROUD (1900-1936)

symphony in a
brno   brno state   cd: praga PR 250 083
1966   philharmonic

CESAR FRANCK (1822-1890)

symphony in d minor

walthamstow 11 october 1946	paris conservatoire orchestra	78: decca K 1639-1642 78: london (usa) LA 110 45: london (usa) EDA 36 lp: decca LXT 2692/ACL 13 lp: london (usa) LLP 464 cd: dante LYS 409
boston 11 march 1957	boston symphony	lp: victor LM 2131/LSC 2131/RB 16306 SB 2009/VIC 1034/VICS 1034 cd: rca/bmg 74321 740172/74321 292562
prague 17 may 1957	czech philharmonic	vhs video: teldec 4509 975106 dvd video: teldec 0927 426682 *rehearsal and performance extracts only*
tanglewood 5 august 1961	boston symphony	cd: music and arts CD 236
rotterdam september- november 1966	rotterdam philharmonic	lp: concert hall SMSA 2519 lp: musidisc FC 411 cd: accord 22.0272 cd: scribendum SC 012
montreal 20 september 1967	orchestre national	cd: accord 20.0532

franck variations symphoniques pour piano et orchestre

walthamstow 11 october 1946	paris conservatoire orchestra joyce, piano	78: decca K 1587-1588 45: london (usa) EDA 35 lp: decca LXT 2692/ACL 13 lp: london (usa) LLP 464 cd: dante LYS 409
tanglewood 1 august 1965	boston symphony henriot-schweitzer, piano	cd: boston symphony orchestra BSOCD 4
boston 7 november 1961	boston symphony perlemuter, piano	cd: music and arts CD 236

le chasseur maudit

boston 10 october 1959	boston symphony	cd: music and arts CD 236
boston 26 february 1962	boston symphony	lp: victor LM 2647/LSC 2647/RB 6528/ SB 6528 cd: rca/bmg 74321 292562

ALEXEI HAIEFF (born 1914)

symphony no 2
boston   boston   lp: victor LM 2352/LSC 2352
30 november   symphony
1958

ERNESTO HALFFTER (1905-1989)

rapsodie portugaise pour piano et orchestre
paris   conservatoire   78: columbia (france) LFX 629-630
27 october   orchestra   cd: classical record ACR 43-44
1941   doyen, piano   cd: dante LYS 357
                                recording completed on 31 march 1942

GEORGE FRIDERIC HANDEL (1685-1759)

water music, suite arranged by harty
boston   boston   45: victor WDM 7009
26 december   symphony   lp: victor LM 7009
1950

boston   boston   cd: boston symphony orchestra BSOCD 1
16 february   symphony
1962

paris   orchestre   cd: classical society CSCD 116
28 august   national
1964

FRANZ JOSEF HAYDN (1732-1809)

symphony no 102
moscow	boston	cd: SMC 100
9 september	symphony	*recording incomplete*
1956		

symphony no 103 "drum roll"
boston	boston	45: victor WDM 1621
26-27	symphony	lp: victor LM 1200
december		
1950		

symphony no 104 "london"
boston	boston	78: victor M 1476
10-11	symphony	45: victor WDM 1476
april		lp: victor LM 49/LM 9034
1950		

sinfonia concertante in b flat
paris	conservatoire	78: oiseau lyre 83-85
october	orchestra	cd: classical record ACR 43-44
1943	charmy, violin	cd: dante LYS 306
	navarra, cello	
	morel, oboe	
	oubrados,	
	bassoon	

in conductors on record (gollancz 1982) john holmes mentions a recording by munch of haydn symphony no 45 "farewell", but it is thought that this may be a confusion with one by karl münchinger

ARTHUR HONEGGER (1892-1955)

symphony no 1
paris	orchestre	cd: disques montaigne TCE 8730
5 june	national	cd: valois V 4830
1962		cd: living stage LS 1042

symphony no 2
paris	conservatoire	78: hmv (france) W 1600-1602
15-16	orchestra	lp: hmv (france) FJLP 5026
october		cd: dante LYS 292
1942		*recording completed on 1 march 1944*
boston	boston	lp: victor LM 1868
1956	symphony	lp: victor (france) A 630275
		lp: victor (italy) A12R 0115
prague	czech	cd: multisonic 310 0202
17 may	philharmonic	cd: living stage LS 1042
1957		
san sebastian	orchestre	cd: disques montaigne MUN 2051
1 september	national	cd: valois V 4831
1964		
paris	orchestre	lp: emi ASD 2467/SME 91796
28 october	de paris	lp: angel 36585
1967		cd: emi CMS 769 9572

honegger **symphony no 3 "liturgique"**
prague	boston	cd: multisonic 310 0252
11 september	symphony	cd: living stage LS 1042
1956		

symphony no 4 "deliciae basiliensis"
paris	orchestre	lp: erato STU 70400
june	national	cd: erato 2292 456892
1967		

symphony no 5 "di tre re"
boston	boston	45: victor WDM 1741
27 october	symphony	lp: victor LM 1741
1952		lp: victor (italy) A12R 0110
		lp: hmv (france) FALP 169
		cd: rca/bmg 09026 606852
helsinki	orchestre	cd: disques montaigne MUN 2051
11 june	national	cd: valois V 4831
1964		

honegger **pastorale d'été/3 mouvements symphoniques**
basel	orchestre	cd: disques montaigne MUN 2051
8 june	national	cd: valois V 4831
1962		

le chant de nigamon
paris	orchestre	cd: disques montaigne MUN 2031
5 june	national	cd: valois V 4831
1962		

la danse des morts, oratorio
paris	conservatoire	78: hmv (france) DB 5135-5137
2 march	orchestra	lp: hmv (france) FJLP 5026
1942	gouverne choir	cd: dante LYS 292
	rabier	
	schenneberg	
	panzéra	
	barrault, narrator	

in conductors on record (gollancz 1982) john holmes mentions a 78rpm recording for odeon (also issued by american decca) of excerpts from le roi david: this is conducted by one "f.münch", but uses the municipal orchestra and chorus of strassburg, where munch had been born and led the orchestra before going to leipzig in 1926

JACQUES IBERT (1890-1962)

escales, poeme symphonique
boston	boston	lp: victor LM 2111/LSC 2111
10 december	symphony	cd: rca/bmg 09026 615002
1956		

VINCENT D'INDY (1851-1931)

symphonie sur un chant montagnard francais "symphonie cévénole"

new york	new york	cd: dante LYS 543
19 december	philharmonic	
1948	casadesus, piano	

new york	new york	78: columbia (usa) M 911
20 december	philharmonic	lp: columbia 33CX 1118
1948	casadesus, piano	lp: columbia (france) FCX 119
		lp: columbia (usa) ML 4298

boston	boston	lp: victor LM 2271/LSC 2271/SB 2053
28 march	symphony	cd: rca/bmg RD 68052/09026 625822
1958	henriot-schweitzer, piano	

fervaal, prélude

london	paris	78: decca K 1718
4 october	conservatoire	78: london (usa) LA 198
1947	orchestra	cd: dante LYS 409

ANDRE JOLIVET (1905-1974)

trois complaintes du soldat vaincu, pour voix et orchestre
paris	conservatoire	78: hmv (france) DB 11158-11159
29 october	orchestra	cd: classical record ACR 40-41
1943	bernac	*recording completed on 1 march 1944*

EDOUARD LALO (1823-1892)

cello concerto
paris	lamoureux	lp: erato STU 70255
april	orchestra	cd: erato 2292 456882
1965	navarra, cello	

le roi d'ys, overture
boston	boston	45: victor WDM 1700
27 december	symphony	lp: victor LM 1700
1950		lp: hmv ALP 1245

FRANZ LISZT (1811-1886)

piano concerto no 1
paris	conservatoire	78: pathé PDT 49-50
7 november	orchestra	
1941	benvente, piano	

piano concerto no 2
new york	new york	cd: dante LYS 543
19 december	philharmonic	
1948	casadesus, piano	

GUSTAV MAHLER (1860-1911)

kindertotenlieder
boston   boston   lp: victor LM 2371/LSC 2371/AGL1-1338
28 december   symphony
1958   forrester

lieder eines fahrenden gesellen
boston   boston   lp: victor LM 2371/LSC 2371/AGL1-1338
29 december   symphony
1958   forrester

BOHUSLAV MARTINU (1890-1959)

symphony no 6 "fantaisies symphoniques"
boston   boston   lp: victor LM 2083/RB 16030/AGL1-3794
23 april   symphony   cd: emi CZS 575 4772
1956

prague   prague radio   cd: panton 811 1222
27 march   orchestra
1957

FELIX MENDELSSOHN-BARTHOLDY (1809-1847)

symphony no 3 "scotch"
boston	boston	lp: victor LM 2520/LSC 2520/RB 16258/
7 december	symphony	SB 2129
1959		*also re-issued on cd by rca/bmg*

symphony no 4 "italian"
boston	boston	lp: victor LM 2221/LSC 2221/VIC 1293/
18 february	symphony	VICS 1293
1958		cd: rca/bmg 09026 680902

symphony no 5 "reformation"
london	paris	78: decca K 1715-1718
29-30	conservatoire	78: london (usa) LA 198
september	orchestra	lp: london (usa) LLP 119
1947		cd: dante LYS 478

boston	boston	lp: victor LM 2221/LSC 2221/VIC 1293/
28 october	symphony	VICS 1293
1957		*also re-issued on cd by rca/bmg*

violin concerto
boston	boston	lp: victor LM 2314/LSC 2314/RB 16182/
23 february	symphony	SB 2066
1959	heifetz, violin	cd: rca/bmg RD 59332/09026 617432/
		09026 617792/09026 689802

boston	boston	lp: victor VIC 1033/VICS 1033
24 december	symphony	
1960	laredo, violin	

MENDELSSOHN
SYMPHONY No. 4 "ITALIAN"
SYMPHONY No. 5 "REFORMATION"
Munch: Boston Symphony

Victrola STEREO
VICS 1293

mendelssohn **capriccio brillant for piano and orchestra**
boston   boston   lp: victor LM 2468/LSC 2468/VIC 1030/
14 march   symphony   VICS 1030
1960   graffman, piano

scherzo/octet for strings
boston   boston   lp: victor LM 2520/LSC 2520/RB 16258/
22 february   symphony   SB 2129
1960   cd: emi CZS 575 4772
                                   emi re-issue is dated 7 march 1960

GIAN CARLO MENOTTI (born 1911)

violin concerto
boston   boston   lp: victor LM 1868
8 november   symphony   lp: victor (france) A 630275
1954   spivakovsky,   lp: victor (italy) A12R 0115
                 violin

CHARLES MUNCH

conducts

THE BOSTON SYMPHONY ORCHESTRA

on RCA VICTOR RECORDS

Elgar
INTRODUCTION AND ALLEGRO FOR STRINGS
together with *Tchaikovsky* **Serenade for strings**
and *Barber* **Adagio for strings**
Ⓜ RB 16025

Ravel
DAPHNIS ET CHLOE - Ballet
Ⓢ SB 2137   Ⓜ RB 16266

Brahms
SYMPHONY No. 4 IN E MINOR
Ⓢ SB 2060   Ⓜ RB 16177

STEREO OR MONO RECORDS

DARIUS MILHAUD (1892-1974)

suite provencale
boston	boston	lp: victor LD 2625/LDS 2625/RB 6511/
13 march	symphony	SB 6511
1961		cd: rca/bmg 09026 606852

la création du monde, ballet
boston	boston	lp: victor LD 2625/LDS 2625/RB 6511/
21 november	symphony	SB 6511
1960		cd: rca/bmg 09026 606852

RAYMOND MONTBRUN (born 1918)

mélodies
paris	conservatoire	78: action artistique AA 9
january	orchestra	
1943		

WOLFGANG AMADEUS MOZART (1756-1791)

symphony no 35 "haffner"
new york 19 december 1948	new york philharmonic	cd: dante LYS 543

piano concerto no 20 k466
paris 23 december 1941	conservatoire orchestra doyen, piano	78: hmv (france) W 1524-1527 cd: classical record ACR 43-44 cd: dante LYS 400 *recording completed on 2 february 1942*
boston 9 november 1956	boston symphony haskil, piano	lp: rococo 2086 cd: music and arts CD 715/CD 1096

piano concerto no 21 k467
new york 20 december 1948	new york philharmonic casadesus, piano	78: columbia LX 1412-1415 78: columbia (usa) M 866 lp: columbia 33C 1024 lp: columbia (france) 33FC 1009 lp: columbia (italy) 33QC 5016 lp: columbia (germany) 33WC 1024 lp: columbia (usa) ML 2067/ML 4791 lp: philips A01291L

piano concerto no 23 k488
montreux 15 september 1959	orchestre national haskil, piano	cd: music and arts CD 922

mozart **violin concerto no 5 k219**
paris	conservatoire	78: hmv (france) DB 5142-5144
6 january	orchestra	lp: hmv (france) FJLP 5015
1941	thibaud, violin	cd: biddulph LAB 114

violin concerto no 7 k271a
paris	orchestra	78: pathé PDT 143-146
14-15	d.soriano,	
march	violin	
1939		

clarinet concerto
tanglewood	boston	lp: victor LM 2073/RB 16013/VICS 1402
9 july	symphony	lp: rca camden classics CCV 5006
1956	goodman,	cd: rca/bmg RD 85272/09026 688042/
	clarinet	74321 246982

adagio and fugue in c minor
paris	conservatoire	78: l'oiseau lyre 90
february	orchestra	
1939		

le nozze di figaro, overture
boston	boston	45: victor WDM 7009
25 april	symphony	lp: victor LM 7009
1951		

MODEST MUSSORGSKY (1839-1881)

khovantschina, entr'acte and dance of the persian slaves
paris	orchestre	lp: concert hall SMSA 2518
october-	national	lp: musidisc FC 439
november		cd: scribendum SC 012
1966		

JACQUES OFFENBACH (1819-1880)

gaité parisienne, ballet arranged by rosenthal
london	new	lp: decca LK 4767/PFS 4096/VIV 60
10-11	philharmonia	lp: london (usa) SPC 21011
december		cd: decca 443 0332
1965		

WALTER PISTON (1894-1976)

symphony no 6
boston	boston	lp: victor LM 2083/RB 16030/AGL1-2445
12-14	symphony	
march		
1956		

FRANCIS POULENC (1899-1963)

organ concerto
boston	boston	lp: victor LM 2567/LSC 2567/RB 16278/
9 october	symphony	SB 2147
1960	zamkochian,	cd: rca/bmg RD 57502/09026 647402
	organ	

SERGE PROKOFIEV (1891-1953)

symphony no 1 "classical"
london	paris	78: decca K 1756-1757
4 october	conservatoire	78: london (usa) LA 178
1947	orchestra	45: london (usa) EDA 107
		lp: london (usa) LLP 169
		cd: dante LYS 520

piano concerto no 2
boston	boston	lp: victor LM 2197/LSC 2197/VIC 1071/
13 february	symphony	VICS 1071
1957	henriot-	
	schweitzer,	
	piano	

violin concerto no 2
boston	boston	lp: victor LM 2314/LSC 2314/RB 16182/
24-25	symphony	SB 2066
february	heifetz, violin	cd: rca/bmg RCD 18019/09026 617442/
1959		09026 617792

romeo and juliet, excerpts from the ballet
boston	boston	lp: victor LM 2110/LSC 2110/RE 25001/
11-13	symphony	VIC 1412/VICS 1412
february		cd: emi CZS 575 4772
1957		

SERGEI RACHMANINOV (1873-1943)

piano concerto no 3

boston	boston	lp: victor LM 2237/LSC 2237/VIC 1032
24 december	symphony	cd: rca/bmg VD 60540/09026 605402/
1957	janis, piano	09026 687622

JEAN-PHILIPPE RAMEAU (1683-1764)

dardanus, ballet suite arranged by d'indy

chicago	chicago	cd: chicago symphony orchestra
27 february	symphony	CSOCD 0001
1963		vhs video: video artists international
		VAI 69605
		dvd video: video artists international
		VAIDVD 4226

MAURICE RAVEL (1875-1937)

piano concerto in g

paris 31 may 1949	conservatoire orchestra henriot- schweitzer, piano	lp: decca LXT 2565 lp: london (usa) LLP 76
boston 28 march 1958	boston symphony henriot- schweitzer, piano	lp: victor LM 2271/LSC 2271/SB 2053/ VIC 1071/VICS 1071
paris 26-28 september 1968	orchestre de paris henriot- schweitzer, piano	lp: emi ASD 2467/SME 91796 lp: angel 36585 cd: emi CMS 769 9572

ravel **piano concerto for the left hand**

paris	conservatoire	78: grammophon 566192-566193/
1938	orchestra	67192-67193
	blancard, piano	78: fonit 91077-91078
		78: decca X 204-205
		78: vox 168
		cd: dante LYS 270
paris	conservatoire	78: hmv DB 3885-3886
12 may	orchestra	78: victor M 629
1939	cortot, piano	lp: toshiba GR 2112
		cd: emi CDH 565 4992
		cd: pearl GEMMCD 9491
		cd: dante LYS 270
		cd: naxos 811.0613
paris	conservatoire	78: columbia (france) LFX 631-633
8 october	orchestra	cd: dante LYS 270
1942	février, piano	

tzigane pour violon et orchestre

new york	new york	lp: discocorp RR 550
2 january	philharmonic	cd: music and arts CD 550/CD 837
1949	neveu, violin	cd: dante LYS 389-390

ravel **daphnis et chloé**

boston 23-24 january 1955	boston symphony new england conservatory chorus	lp: victor LM 1893 lp: victor (france) A 630294 lp: hmv ALP 1374 cd: rca/bmg 09026 680812
boston 26-27 february 1961	boston symphony new england conservatory chorus	lp: victor LM 2568/LSC 2568/RB 16266/ SB 2137 cd: rca/bmg 09028 618462

daphnis et chloé, second suite

walthamstow 9 october 1946	paris conservatoire orchestra	78: decca AK 1584-1586 cd: dutton CDK 1201 cd: dante LYS 269
cambridge mass. 17 april 1962	boston symphony	vhs video: teldec 4509 957103 dvd video: teldec 0927 426682 *excerpts only*
philadelphia 7 march 1963	philadelphia orchestra	cd: philadelphia orchestra POA 100.4
budapest april 1966	hungarian state orchestra	vhs video: teldec 4509 957103 dvd video: teldec 0927 426682 *rehearsal extract only*
paris 21-24 september 1968	orchestre de paris	lp: emi ASD 2497/SME 91795 lp: angel 36584 cd: emi CDC 747 3562/CMS 769 9572 *recording completed on 3 october 1968*

ravel **nocturne et danse guerriere/daphnis et chloé**

walthamstow	paris	78: decca AK 1584-1585
9 october	conservatoire	78: london (usa) LA 225
1946	orchestra	45: london (usa) EDA 29
		cd: dutton CDK 1201
		cd: dante LYS 269

boléro

walthamstow	paris	78: decca K 1637-1638
10 october	conservatoire	45: london (usa) EDA 33
1946	orchestra	lp: decca LXT 2677
		lp: london (usa) LLP 22/LLP 466
		cd: dante LYS 269
boston	boston	lp: victor LM 1984/LSC 1984/RB 16130
23 january	symphony	SB 2019/VIC 1041/VICS 1041
1956		cd: rca/bmg 09026 619562
boston	boston	lp: victor LM 2664/LSC 2664/RB 6556/
26 march	symphony	SB 6556
1962		cd: rca/bmg RD 65222
paris	orchestre	lp: emi ASD 2497/SME 91795
21-24	de paris	lp: angel 36584
september		cd: emi CDC 747 3562/CMS 769 9572
1968		*recording completed on 3 october 1968*

ma mere l'oye

boston	boston	lp: victor LM 2292/LSC 2292/RB 16155/
19 february	symphony	SB 2041/VIC 1060/VICS 1060
1957		cd: rca/bmg 09026 652222/74321 292572

ravel **pavane pour une infante défunte**

paris 3 march 1942	conservatoire orchestra	78: hmv (france) W 1558 cd: classical record ACR 40-41 cd: dante LYS 269
boston 27 october 1952	boston symphony	45: victor ERB 7016 lp: victor LM 1741/LRM 7016 lp: victor (italy) A12R 0110
boston 26 march 1962	boston symphony	lp: victor LM 2664/LSC 2664/RB 6556/ SB 6556 cd: rca/bmg RD 65222
paris 21-24 september 1968	orchestre de paris	lp: emi ASD 2497/SME 91796 lp: angel 3768 cd: emi CDC 747 3562/CMS 769 9572

rapsodie espagnole

paris 16 april 1941	conservatoire orchestra	hmv (france) unpublished
boston 26 december 1950	boston symphony	45: victor WDM 1700/ERB 7016 lp: victor LM 1700/LRM 7016 lp: hmv ALP 1245
boston 23 january 1956	boston symphony	lp: victor LM 1984/LSC 1984/RB 16130/ SB 2019/VIC 1041/VICS 1041 cd: rca/bmg RD 65222/09026 619562
paris 21-24 september 1968	orchestre de paris	lp: emi ASD 2497/SME 91795 lp: angel 36584 cd: emi CDC 747 3562/CMS 769 9572 *recording completed on 3 october 1968*

ravel **la valse**

paris 3 march 1942	conservatoire orchestra	78: hmv (france) W 1557-1558 cd: classical record ACR 40-41 cd: dante LYS 269
boston 11 april 1950	boston symphony	78: victor 12-1207 45: victor WDM 1700/ERB 7016/49-1213 45: hmv (france) 7RF 257 lp: victor LM 1700/LRM 7016/LM 6113 lp: victor (italy) A12R 0130 lp: victor (france) A 630217 lp: hmv ALP 1245
boston 5 december 1955	boston symphony	lp: victor LM 1984/LSC 1984/RB 16130/ SB 2019 cd: rca/bmg 09026 619562
boston 1 december 1958	boston symphony	victor unpublished
boston 26 march 1962	boston symphony	lp: victor LM 2664/LSC 2664/RB 6556/ SB 6556 cd: rca/bmg RD 65222
tokyo 28 december 1962	tokyo philharmonic	cd: japan P23 G541

chicago
27 february
1963
	chicago
	symphony
		vhs video: video artists international 69605
		    VAI 69605
		dvd video: video artists international
		    VAIDVD 4226

valses nobles et sentimentales

philadelphia 14 march 1963	philadelphia orchestra	lp: columbia (usa) ML 5923/MS 6523 cd: sony SBK 48163

OTTORINO RESPIGHI (1879-1936)

fontane di roma
london	new	lp: decca PFS 4131
4-5	philharmonia	lp: london (usa) SPC 21024
january		cd: decca 444 1062
1967		

pini di roma
london	new	lp: decca PFS 4131
4-5	philharmonia	lp: london (usa) SPC 21024
january		cd: decca 444 1062
1967		

NIKOLAI RIMSKY-KORSAKOV (1844-1908)

russian easter festival overture
paris	orchestre	lp: concert hall SMSA 2511
october-	national	lp: musidisc FC 439
november		cd: fnac 642330
1966		cd: scribendum SC 012

le coq d'or, introduction and cortege
paris	orchestre	lp: concert hall SMSA 2511
october-	national	lp: musidisc FC 439
november		cd: fnac 642330
1966		cd: scribendum SC 012

JEAN RIVIER (1896-1987)

ouverture pour une opérette imaginaire
paris	conservatoire	78: action artistique AA 35
november	orchestra	
1943		

ALBERT ROUSSEL (1869-1937)

symphony no 3

edinburgh	orchestre	cd: disques montaigne MUN 2041
19 august	national	cd: valois V 4832
1964		

paris	lamoureux	lp: erato STU 70256
april	orchestra	lp: world records T 649/ST 649
1965		cd: erato 2292 456872/0927 467302

chicago	chicago	cd: chicago symphony orchestra CSOCD 0009
16-18	symphony	
february		
1967		

symphony no 4

paris	lamoureux	lp: erato STU 70256
april	orchestra	lp: world records T 649/ST 649
1965		cd: erato 2292 456872/0927 467302

besancon	orchestre	cd: disques montaigne MUN 2041
13 september	national	cd: valois V 4832
1966		

le festin de l'araignée, ballet

london	london	78: decca K 1691-1692
6 june	philharmonic	45: london (usa) EDA 44
1947		cd: dante LYS 438

petite suite

paris	conservatoire	78: decca K 1643-1644
9 october	orchestra	45: london (usa) EDA 37
1946		cd: dante LYS 438

roussel suite in f

london 2-6 june 1947	london philharmonic	78: decca K 1772-1773/AX 317-318 cd: dante LYS 438
strassburg 15 june 1958	orchestre national	cd: ina EURM 2009
paris april 1965	lamoureux orchestra	lp: erato STU 70278

bacchus et ariane, suite no 2

boston 27 october 1952	boston symphony	45: victor WDM 1741 lp: victor LM 1741/LM 6113 lp: victor (italy) A12R 0110/A12R 0130 lp: victor (france) A 630217 lp: hmv (france) FALP 169 cd: rca/bmg 09026 614852
paris 10 december 1961	orchestre national	lp: véga C30 A351
paris 5 june 1962	orchestre national	cd: disques montaigne TCE 8730/MUN 2051 cd: valois V 4831 cd: living stage LS 1042
tokyo 20 december 1962	tokyo philharmonic	cd: japan P23 G541
paris 22 november 1966	orchestre national	cd: disques montaigne MUN 2041 cd: valois V 4832

CAMILLE SAINT-SAENS (1835-1921)

symphony no 3 "organ"

new york 10 november 1947	new york philharmonic nies-berger, organ	78: columbia (france) LFX 901-904 78: columbia (italy) GQX 11358-11361 78: columbia (holland) LHX 8003-8006 78: columbia (usa) M 747 lp: columbia 33CX 1116 lp: columbia (france) 33FCX 166 lp: columbia (italy) 33QCX 166 lp: columbia (usa) ML 4120

boston
5-6
april
1959
	boston
	symphony
	zamkochian,
	organ
		lp: victor LM 2341/LSC 2341/RB 16214/
		    SB 2089
		cd: rca/bmg RD 57502/09026 614002/
		    09026 615002

piano concerto no 4

london 9 july 1935	orchestra cortot, piano	78: hmv DB 2577-2579 78: victor M 367 lp: rococo 2040 cd: pearl GEMMCD 9491 cd: dante LYS 306 cd: philips 456 7542 cd: naxos 811.0612
boston 24 november 1954	boston symphony brailowsky, piano	lp: victor LM 1871 lp: victor (france) A 630242 lp: hmv ALP 1321 cd: rca/bmg 09026 681852

saint-saens **introduction et rondo capriccioso pour violon et orchestra**

boston	boston	lp: victor LM 1988/RB 16166/
14 december	symphony	VIC 1058/VICS 1058
1955	oistrakh, violin	cd: rca/bmg GD 60683/09026 606832

cello concerto no 1

paris	lamoureux	lp: erato STU 70255
april	orchestra	cd: erato 2292 456882
1965	navarra, cello	

danse macabre

amsterdam	concertgebouw	78: decca K 2069
15 september	orchestra	78: decca (holland) X 10245
1948		78: london (usa) T 5120

la princesse jaune, overture

boston	boston	45: victor WDM 1700/ERA 68
18 january	symphony	lp: victor LM 1700
1951		lp: hmv ALP 1245
		cd: emi CZS 575 4772

le rouet d'omphale

walthamstow	paris	78: decca K 1695
11 october	conservatoire	cd: dante LYS 409
1946	orchestra	

boston	boston	lp: victor LM 2292/LSC 2292/RB 16155/
4 november	symphony	SB 2041
1957		cd: rca/bmg 09026 614002

GUSTAVE SAMAZEUILH (1887-1967)

le cercle des heures, pour alto et orchestre
paris	conservatoire	78: hmv (france) W 1564
21 april	orchestra	cd: classical record ACR 43-44
1943	schenneberg	

nuit, poeme pour orchestre
paris	conservatoire	78: hmv (france) W 1563
21 april	orchestra	cd: classical record ACR 43-44
1943		

FLORENT SCHMITT (1870-1958)

symphony no 2
strassburg	orchestre	cd: ina EURM 2009
15 june	national	
1958		

FRANZ SCHUBERT (1797-1828)

symphony no 2
boston	boston	78: victor M 1448
20 december	symphony	45: victor WDM 1448
1949		lp: victor LM 41/LM 9032/VIC 1018
		lp: hmv ALP 1061
		lp: hmv (italy) QALP 10031

boston	boston	lp: victor LM 2522/LSC 2522/RB 6508/
7 march	symphony	SB 6508
1960		

symphony no 8 "unfinished"
boston	boston	lp: victor LM 1923/VIC 1035/VICS 1035
2 may	symphony	cd: rca/bmg 09026 615512
1955		

symphony no 9 "great"
boston	boston	lp: victor LM 2344/LSC 2344/RB 16210/
19 november	symphony	SB 2085/VIC 1126/VICS 1126/
1958		26.41388/AGL1-5064
		lp: rca camden classics CCV 5054
		cd: rca/bmg VD 60792/VD 60807/
		09026 626782

ROBERT SCHUMANN (1810-1856)

symphony no 1 "spring"
boston	boston	45: victor WDM 1608
25 april	symphony	lp: victor LM 1190
1951		lp: hmv ALP 1203
		lp: hmv (france) FALP 175
		lp: hmv (italy) QALP 175

boston	boston	lp: victor LM 2474/LSC 2474/RB 16255/ SB 2126
5 october	symphony	
1959		cd: rca/bmg 09026 604882

symphony no 4
london	london	78: decca AK 2022-2024
4 june	philharmonic	45: london (usa) EDA 61
1947		

stuttgart	orchestre	cd: disques montaigne MUN 2021
19 january	national	cd: valois V 4827
1966		

schumann **piano concerto**
walthamstow	paris	decca unpublished
8 october	conservatoire	
1946	orchestra	
	henriot-	
	schweitzer, piano	

boston	boston	victor unpublished
6 october	symphony	
1958	cliburn, piano	

genoveva overture
boston	boston	45: victor WDM 7009
18 january	symphony	lp: victor LM 7009
1951		cd: rca/bmg 09026 606822

manfred overture
boston	boston	lp: victor LM 2474/LSC 2474/RB 16255/
5 october	symphony	SB 2126
1959		cd: rca/bmg 74321 212842

JEAN SIBELIUS (1865-1957)

swan of tuonela/4 legends
helsinki	orchestre	cd: disques montaigne MUN 2031
11 june	national	
1964		

the return of lemminkainen/4 legends
helsinki	orchestre	cd: disques montaigne MUN 2031
11 june	national	
1964		

BEDRICH SMETANA (1824-1884)

vltava/ma vlast
paris　　　　　　orchestre　　　　lp: concert hall SMSA 2761
february　　　　national
1968

JOHN STAFFORD SMITH (1750-1836)

the star-spangled banner, march
boston　　　　　boston　　　　　lp: american heritage foundation
28 october　　　symphony　　　　　AHF 1003
1957

RICHARD STRAUSS (1864-1949)

don quixote
boston	boston	lp: victor LM 1781
17 august	symphony	lp: victor (france) A 630206
1953	piatigorsky,	lp: victor (italy) A12R 0047
	cello	lp: hmv ALP 1211
		cd: rca/bmg 09026 614852

till eulenspiegels lustige streiche
boston	boston	lp: victor LM 2565/LSC 2565
20 march	symphony	
1961		

IGOR STRAVINSKY (1882-1971)

jeu de cartes, ballet
boston	boston	lp: victor LM 2567/LSC 2567/RB 16278/
7 november	symphony	SB 2147
1960		

PIOTR TCHAIKOVSKY (1840-1893)

symphony no 4
boston	boston	lp: victor LM 1953/RB 16012/VIC 1100
7 november	symphony	cd: victor (japan) BVCC 37342
1955		

symphony no 6 "pathétique"
paris	conservatoire	78: decca K 1968-1973
24-27	orchestra	lp: decca LXT 2544/ACL 20
may		lp: london (usa) LLP 257
1948		cd: dante LYS 520

boston	boston	lp: victor LM 2683/LSC 2683/RB 6550/
12 march	symphony	SB 6550
1962		cd: rca/bmg 09026 615632

piano concerto no 1
paris	conservatoire	78: columbia (france) LFX 595-598
17-21	orchestra	cd: dante LYS 400
april	konstantinoff,	
1941	piano	

tchaikovsky **violin concerto**

boston 29 march 1953	boston symphony milstein, violin	lp: victor LM 1760/VIC 1003 lp: victor (france) A 630243 lp: hmv (france) FBLP 1047 cd: victor (japan) BVCC 37348
boston 9 february 1959	boston symphony szeryng, violin	lp: victor LM 2363/LSC 2363/RB 16204/ SB 2080/VIC 1037/VICS 1037

serenade for strings

boston 3 april 1957	boston symphony	lp: victor LM 2105/LSC 2105/RB 16025 cd: rca/bmg 09026 614242

francesca da rimini

boston 23 april 1956	boston symphony	lp: victor LM 2043/VIC 1197/VICS 1197 lp: rca camden classics CCV 5013
walthamstow 5 april 1963	royal philharmonic	lp: readers digest RD 47/RDS 47 cd: chesky CD 7

romeo and juliet

boston 12 march 1956	boston symphony	lp: victor LM 2043/VIC 1197/VICS 1197 lp: rca camden classics CCV 5013
boston 3 april 1961	boston symphony	lp: victor LM 2565/LSC 2565 cd: rca/bmg 09026 615632

ANTONIO VIVALDI (1678-1741)

violin concerto op 3 no 9, arranged by dandelot
paris orchestra 78: pathé PDT 154-155
9 may d.soriano,
1939 violin

RICHARD WAGNER (1813-1883)

siegfried's rhine journey/götterdämmerung
boston	boston	lp: victor LM 2219/LSC 2219/RB 16034/
1 april	symphony	VIC 1065/VICS 1065
1957		lp: rca camden classics CCV 5044

brünnhilde's immolation/götterdämmerung
boston	boston	lp: victor LM 2255/LSC 2255/
25 november	symphony	VIC 1191/VICS 1191
1957	farrell	cd: rca/bmg GD 60686/09026 606862

overture and venusberg music/tannhäuser
boston	boston	lp: victor LM 2219/LSC 2219/RB 16034/
1 april	symphony	VIC 1065/VICS 1065
1957		lp: rca camden classics CCV 5044
		cd: rca/bmg GD 60686/09026 606862

prelude and liebestod/tristan und isolde
boston	boston	lp: victor LM 2255/LSC 2255/
25 november	symphony	VIC 1191/VICS 1191
1957	farrell	cd: rca/bmg GD 60686/09026 606862

magic fire music/die walküre
boston	boston	lp: victor LM 2219/LSC 2219/RB 16034/
1 april	symphony	VIC 1065/VICS 1065
1957		lp: rca camden classics CCV 5044
		cd: rca/bmg GD 60686/09026 606862

WILLIAM WALTON (1902-1983)

cello concerto
boston	boston	lp: victor LM 2109/LSC 2109/RB 16027
30 january	symphony	cd: rca/bmg 74321 292482
1957	piatigorsky, cello	

CHARLES WIDOR (1845-1937)

fantaisie pour piano et orchestre
paris	conservatoire	78: grammophon 566205-566206
1938	orchestra	cd: dante LYS 306
	herrenschmidt, piano	

paul paray
1886-1979

ADOLPHE ADAM (1803-1856)

si j'étais roi, overture
detroit   detroit
19 november   symphony
1960

lp: mercury MG 50247/MG 50324/
    MG 50377/SR 90247/SR 90324/
    SR 90377
lp: philips classical favourites GL 5830/
    SGL 5830
cd: philips mercury 434 3322

DANIEL AUBER (1782-1871)

le cheval de bronze, overture
detroit   detroit
4 april   symphony
1959

45: mercury XEP 9072/SEX 15019
lp: mercury MG 50215/MG 50377/
    SR 90215/SR 90377/MMA 11099/
    AMS 16045
lp: mercury wing MGW 14058/SRW 18058
lp: philips classical favourites GL 5830/
    SGL 5830
cd: philips mercury 434 3092

les diamants de la couronne, overture
detroit   detroit
19 november   symphony
1960

45: mercury XEP 9072
lp: mercury MG 50215/MG 50324/
    MG 50377/SR 90247/SR 90324/
    SR 90377
lp: mercury wing MGW 14058/SEW 18058
lp: philips classical favourites GL 5830/
    SGL 5830
lp: mercury golden imports SRI 75077
cd: philips mercury 432 0142

auber **fra diavolo, overture**
detroit	detroit	45: mercury XEP 9111
4 april	symphony	lp: mercury MG 50215/MG 50377/ SR 90215/SR 90377/MMA 11099/ AMS 16045
1959		lp: mercury wing MGW 14058/SRW 18058
		cd: philips mercury 434 3092

la muette de portici, overture
detroit	detroit	45: mercury XEP 9072/SEX 15019
4 april	symphony	lp: mercury MG 50215/SR 90215/ MMA 11099/AMS 16045
1959		cd: philips mercury 434 3092

HENRY BARRAUD (1900-1997)

offrande a une ombre
detroit	detroit	lp: mercury MG 50145/MMA 11044
19 march	symphony	cd: philips mercury 434 3892
1957		

LUDWIG VAN BEETHOVEN (1770-1827)

symphony no 1
detroit	detroit	lp: mercury MG 50205/SR 90205/
18 january	symphony	MMA 11090/AMS 16039
1959		lp: mercury wing MGW 14062/SRW 18062
		lp: philips classical favourites GL 5804/ 642 250GL

symphony no 2
detroit	detroit	lp: mercury MG 50205/SR 90205/
18 january	symphony	MMA 11090/AMS 16039
1959		lp: mercury wing MGW 15062/SRW 18062
		lp: philips classical favourites GL 5804/ 642 250GL

symphony no 6 "pastoral"
paris	colonne	78: columbia DX 655-659/DCX 63-67
1945	orchestra	78: columbia (australia) DOX 489-493
		78: columbia (belgium) BFX 8-12
		78: columbia (usa) M 201
detroit	detroit	lp: mercury MG 50045
26 november	symphony	lp: mercury wing MGW 14001/SRW 18001
1954		lp: philips 6747 234
		lp: philips wing WL 1001
		lp: philips pergola 832 027PGY

in conductors on record (gollancz 1982) john holmes refers to a pre-electric recording of the symphony by paray and the colonne orchestra, but this is not mentioned in the orchestra on record 1896-1926 by claude graveley arnold (greenwood press)

symphony no 7
detroit	detroit	lp: mercury MG 50022/MRL 2008/MLP 7502
february	symphony	lp: mercury wing MGW 14007/SRW 18007
1953		lp: philips wing WL 1005

beethoven **symphony no 8**
paris orchestre lp: carthagene 731 888
14 november national
1973

piano concerto in e flat woO 4
paris pro musica 78: grammophon 566 292-566 294
1946-1947 chamber 78: vox (usa) 647
 orchestra lp: vox PLP 6470
 frugoni, piano

turkish march/die ruinen von athen
paris colonne 78: columbia DX 659/DCX 67
1945 orchestra 78: columbia (australia) DOX 493
 78: columbia (belgium) BFX 12
 78: columbia (usa) M 201

HECTOR BERLIOZ (1803-1869)

symphonie fantastique
paris	colonne	lp: vox PL 6950
1946-1947	orchestra	

detroit	detroit	lp: mercury MG 50254/MG 50375/
28 november	symphony	SR 90254/SR 90375/MMA 11104/
1959		AMS 16055
		lp: mercury wing MGW 14098/SRW 18098
		lp: philips classical favourites GL 5829/
		SGL 5829
		lp: philips mercury 130 504MGY
		cd: philips mercury 434 3282

benvenuto cellini, overture
paris	colonne	78: grammophon 45450
1946-1947	orchestra	

le carnaval romain, overture
detroit	detroit	45: mercury XEP 9075
24 march	symphony	lp: mercury MG 50191/MG 50323/
1958		MG 50359/MG 50375/MG 50376/
		SR 90191/SR 90323/SR 90359/
		SR 90375/SR 90376/SR2-9134/
		AMS 16013
		cd: philips mercury 434 3282

le corsaire, overture
detroit	detroit	45: mercury XEP 9075
24 march	symphony	lp: mercury MG 50191/MG 50323/
1958		MG 50359/MG 50375/MG 50376/
		SR 90191/SR 90323/SR 90359/
		SR 90375/SR 90376/SR2-9134/
		AMS 16013
		cd: philips mercury 434 3282

ROYAL ALBERT HALL

(Manager - C. S. TAYLOR)

TUESDAY, JUNE 26th, 1945, at 7 p.m.

IN AID OF

ST. MARY'S HOSPITAL, LONDON, W.2

YEHUDI MENHUIN

AND THE

LONDON SYMPHONY ORCHESTRA

Leader: GEORGE STRATTON

Conducted by

PAUL PARAY

Sponsored by The Daily Telegraph

Hon. Management: HAROLD HOLT, Ltd.

berlioz **marche hongroise/la damnation de faust**
paris	colonne	78: grammophon 54500
1946-1947	orchestra	

detroit	detroit	45: mercury XEP 9083/SEX 15025
3 april	symphony	lp: mercury MG 50211/MG 50292/
1959		SR 90211/SR 90292/SR2-9131/
		MMA 11130/AMS 16077
		lp: philips classical favourites GL 5837/
		SGL 5837/837 871GY
		cd: philips mercury 434 3282

marche troyenne/les troyens
detroit	detroit	45: mercury XEP 9109
3 april	symphony	lp: mercury MG 50211/MG 50325/
1959		MG 50377/SR 90211/SR 90325/
		SR 90377/MMA 11130/AMS 16077
		lp: philips classical favourites GL 5830/
		GL 5837/SGL 5830/SGL 5837/
		837 871GY
		cd: philips mercury 434 3282

chasse royal et orage/les troyens
detroit	detroit	lp: mercury MG 50318/MG 50375/
17 march	symphony	SR 90318/SR 90375/SR2-9130
1962		cd: philips mercury 432 0142

GEORGES BIZET (1838-1875)

l'arlésienne, suites nos 1 and 2

detroit 8 november 1956	detroit symphony	lp: mercury MG 50135/MG 50374/ SR 90001/SR 90374/MMA 11102/ AMS 16053 lp: mercury wing MGW 14074/SRW 18074 lp: mercury golden imports SRI 75060 lp: philips classical favourites GL 5826/ SGL 5826 cd: philips mercury 434 3212

excerpts
lp: mercury MG 50293/MG 50532/
SR 90293/SR 90532

carmen, suites nos 1 and 2

monte carlo 22-24 may 1979	monte carlo opera orchestra	lp: concert hall SMSA 6506

carmen, suite arranged by paray

detroit 8 november 1956	detroit symphony	45: mercury XEP 9088/SEX 15029 lp: mercury MG 50135/MG 50374/ SR 90001/SR 90374/MMA 11102/ AMS 16053 lp: mercury wing MGW 14074/SRW 18074 lp: mercury golden imports SRI 75060 lp: philips SDAL 502 lp: philips classical favourites GL 5826/ SGL 5926 cd: philips mercury 434 3212

bizet **danse boheme/carmen**
detroit	detroit	lp: mercury MG 50318/SR 90318
17 march	symphony	cd: philips mercury 432 0142
1962		

la jolie fille de perth, suite
monte	monte carlo	lp: concert hall SMSA 6506
carlo	opera orchestra	
22-24		
may		
1977		

patrie, overture
detroit	detroit	45: mercury XEP 9023
24 march	symphony	lp: mercury MG 50191/MG 50323/
1958		MG 50359/MG 50375/MG 50376/
		SR 90191/SR 90323/SR 90359/
		SR 90376/AMS 16013
		lp: mercury wing MGW 14071/SRW 18071
		lp: philips classical favourites GL 5839/
		SGL 5839/837 824GY
		cd: philips mercury 434 3212

FRANCOIS BOIELDIEU (1775-1834)

la dame blanche, overture
detroit detroit
19 november symphony
1960

lp: mercury MG 50247/MG 50324/ MG 50377/SR 90247/SR 90324/ SR 90377
lp: philips classical favourites GL 5830/ SGL 5830
cd: philips mercury 434 3322

JOHANNES BRAHMS (1833-1897)

symphony no 4
detroit detroit
26 march symphony
1955

lp: mercury MG 50057
lp: mercury wing MGW 14003/SRW 18003
lp: philips wing WL 1003
lp: philips fontana special SFL 14070/ 700 184WGY

ERNEST CHAUSSON (1855-1899)

symphony in b flat

detroit 24 march 1956	detroit symphony	lp: mercury MG 50017/MG 50108/ MG 50331/SR 90017/SR 90331/ MMA 11111 lp: mercury golden imports SRI 75029 cd: philips mercury 434 3892

EMANUEL CHABRIER (1841-1894)

bourrée fantastique

detroit 19 march 1957	detroit symphony	lp: mercury MG 50145/MG 50374/ SR 90005/SR 90374/SR2-9127/ MMA 11044 lp: mercury golden imports SRI 75078 lp: philips classical favourites GL 5826/ SGL 5826 cd: philips mercury 434 3032

espana

detroit 25 march 1955	detroit symphony	45: mercury XEP 9066 lp: mercury MG 50056 lp: mercury wing MGW 14009/MGW 14036/ SRW 18009/SRW 18036
detroit 18 november 1960	detroit symphony	lp: mercury MG 50212/MG 50374/ SR 90212/SR 90374 lp: mercury wing MGW 14068/SRW 18068 lp: philips classical favourites GL 5826/ SGL 5826 cd: philips mercury 434 3032
monte carlo october 1969	monte carlo opera orchestra	lp: concert hall SMSA 2663 lp: musidisc FC 440

chabrier **gwendoline overture**
detroit	detroit	lp: mercury MG 50212/MG 50377/ SR 90212/SR 90377
18 november	symphony	
1960		lp: mercury wing MGW 14068/SRW 18068
		lp: mercury golden imports SRI 75078
		lp: philips classical favourites GL 5830/ SGL 5830
		cd: philips mercury 434 3032

joyeuse marche
detroit	detroit	45: mercury XEP 9109
5 april	symphony	lp: mercury MG 50211/MG 50292/ MG 50374/SR 90211/SR 90292/ SR 90374/MMA 11130/AMS 16077
1959		
		lp: mercury golden imports SRI 75078
		lp: philips classical favourites GL 5826/ GL 5837/SGL 5826/SGL 5837/ 837 871GY
		cd: philips mercury 434 3032

suite pastorale
detroit	detroit	lp: mercury MG 50212/SR 90212
18 november	symphony	lp: mercury wing MGW 14068/SRW 18068
1960		lp: mercury golden imports SRI 75029
		cd: philips mercury 434 3032

monte	monte carlo	lp: concert hall SMSA 2663
carlo	opera orchestra	lp: musidisc FC 440
october		
1969		

chabrier **fete polonaise/le roi malgré lui**

detroit	detroit	lp: mercury MG 50212/MG 50339/
18 november	symphony	SR 90212/SR 90339
1960		lp: mercury wing MGW 14068/SRW 18068
		lp: mercury golden imports SRI 75078
		cd: philips mercury 434 3032

danse slave/le roi malgré lui

detroit	detroit	lp: mercury MG 50212/SR 90212
18 november	symphony	lp: mercury wing MGW 14068/SRW 18068
1960		lp: mercury golden imports SRI 75078
		cd: philips mercury 434 3032

JEAN-YVES DANIEL-LESUR (born 1908)

ouverture pour un festival

paris	orchestre	lp: carthagene 731 887
16 may	philharmonique	
1972	de l'ortf	

CLAUDE DEBUSSY (1862-1918)

la mer
detroit	detroit	lp: mercury MG 50010/MG 50372/
4 december	symphony	SR 90010/SR 90372
1955		lp: mercury golden imports SRI 75053
		lp: philips classical favourites GL 5836/
		SGL 5836/837 872GY
		cd: philips mercury 434 3432

trois nocturnes
detroit	detroit	lp: mercury MG 50281/SR 90281
11 march	symphony	lp: mercury golden imports SRI 75100
1961	wayne university	cd: philips mercury 434 3062
	glee club	*nuages*
		lp: mercury SR2-9132
		fetes
		lp: mercury MG 50361/SR 90361

ibéria/images pour orchestre
detroit	detroit	lp: mercury MG 50010/MG 50372/
3 december	symphony	SR 90010/SR 90372
1955		lp: mercury golden imports SRI 75053
		lp: philips classical favourites GL 5836/
		SGL 5836/837 872GY
		cd: philips mercury 434 3432

petite suite, arranged by büsser
detroit	detroit	45: mercury XEP 9094/SEX 15034
3 april	symphony	lp: mercury MG 50213/MG 50372/
1959		SR 90213/SR 90372/SR2-9132/
		MMA 11119/AMS 16066
		lp: mercury wing MGW 14078/SRW 18078
		lp: philips classical favourites GL 5836/
		SGL 5836/837 872GY
		cd: philips mercury 434 3062

debussy **prélude a l'apres-midi d'un faune**

detroit	detroit	lp: mercury MG 50010/MG 50213/
3 december	symphony	MG 50372/SR 90010/SR 90213/
1955		SR 90372/SR2-9127/SR2-9132/
		MMA 1119/AMS 16066

lp: mercury wing MGW 14078/SRW 18078
lp: mercury golden imports SRI 75053
lp: philips 6747 228
lp: philips classical favourites GL 5836/ SGL 5836/837 872GY
cd: philips mercury 434 3432

VINCENT D'INDY (1851-1931)

symphonie cévénole pour piano et orchestre

paris	colonne	78: columbia LX 362-364
uncertain	orchestra	78: columbia (france) LFX 352-354
date	m.long, piano	78: columbia (usa) M 211

PAUL DUKAS (1865-1935)

l'apprenti sorcier

detroit
26-28
december
1953
	detroit
	symphony
		45: mercury XEP 9100
		lp: mercury MG 50035/MRL 2500/
		    MLP 7519/MMA 11096
		lp: mercury wing MGW 14009/SRW 18009
		lp: philips 6870 577
		lp: philips fontana special SFL 14140/
		    700 455WGY
		*additional mercury lp editions contained an
		overdubbed spoken commentary on the work*

monte carlo october 1969	monte carlo opera orchestra	lp: concert hall SMSA 2663 lp: musidisc FC 440

la péri, poeme dansé

paris 1946-1947	colonne orchestra	78: grammophon 566 311-566 313/ 545 000

ANTONIN DVORAK (1841-1904)

symphony no 9 "new world"

detroit 19 february 1960	detroit symphony	lp: mercury MG 50262/SR 90262/ MMA 11132 lp: philips fontana special 130 503MGY cd: philips mercury 434 3172

GABRIEL FAURE (1845-1924)

pavane pour une infante défunte

detroit 7 december 1953	detroit symphony	45: mercury XEP 9066 lp: mercury MG 50029/MRL 2510 lp: mercury wing MGW 14009/SRW 18009
paris 16 may 1972	orchestre philharmonique de l'ortf	lp: carthagene 731 887

pelléas et mélisande, suite

detroit 26-28 december 1953	detroit symphony	45: mercury XEP 9067 lp: mercury MG 50035/MRL 2500/ MLP 7519/MMA 11096 lp: mercury wing MGW 14009/SRW 18009
paris 1971	orchestre philharmonique de l'ortf	unpublished video recording

CESAR FRANCK (1822-1890)

symphony in d minor

detroit	detroit	lp: mercury MG 50023/MLP 7510
february	symphony	lp: mercury wing WL 1002
1953		lp: philips wing MGW 14002/SRW 18002

detroit	detroit	lp: mercury MG 50285/MG 90376/
27 november	symphony	SR 90285/SR 90376
1959		lp: philips classical favourites GL 5833/
		SGL 5833/832 869GY
		lp: philips grandioso 894 088ZKY
		cd: philips mercuy 434 3682
		second movement
		lp: mercury SR2-9128

psyché, 3 movements from the symphonic poem: le sommeil de psyché; psyché enlevée par les zéphyres; psyché et éros

detroit	detroit	lp: mercury MG 50029/MRL 2510/
7 december	symphony	MMA 11088
1953		lp: mercury wing MGW 14036/SRW 18036

paris	orchestre	lp: carthagene 731 887
29 may	philharmonique	
1973	de l'ortf	

CHARLES GOUNOD (1818-1893)

faust, ballet music
detroit	detroit	lp: mercury MG 50318/SR 90318
17 march	symphony	cd: philips mercury 432 0142
1962		

waltz/faust
detroit	detroit	lp: mercury MG 50318/SR 90318/
17 march	symphony	SR2-9127/SR2-9130
1962		lp: mercury wing MGW 14087/SRW 18087
		lp: philips 839 819GY
		cd: philips mercury 432 0142

marche funebre d'une marionette
detroit	detroit	45: mercury XEP 9083
4 april	symphony	lp: mercury MG 50211/MG 50292/
1959		SR 90211/SR 90292/MMA 11130/
		AMS 16077
		lp: philips classical favourites GL 5837/
		SGL 5837/837 871GY
		cd: philips mercury 434 3322

FRANZ JOSEF HAYDN (1732-1809)

symphony no 96 "miracle"
detroit 21 october 1956	detroit symphony	mercury unpublished

detroit 18-19 march 1957	detroit symphony	lp: mercury MG 50129/SR 90129/ MMA 11101/AMS 16052 lp: mercury wing MGW 14046/SRW 18046 lp: philips wing WL 1049 lp: philips pergola 832 031PGY cd: philips mercury 434 3962

LOUIS-FERDINAND HEROLD (1791-1833)

zampa, overture

detroit
19 november
1960
	detroit
	symphony
		lp: mercury MG 50247/MG 50324/
		    MG 50377/SR 90247/SR 90324/
		    SR 90377
		lp: mercury golden imports SRI 75077
		lp: philips DL 88028
		lp: philips classical favourites GL 5830/
		    SGL 5830
		cd: philips mercury 432 0142

JACQUES IBERT (1890-1962)

escales

detroit	detroit	lp: mercury MG 50056/MMA 11111
25 march	symphony	lp: mercury wing MGW 14030/SRW 18030
1955		
detroit	detroit	lp: mercury MG 50313/SR 90313/
18 march	symphony	lp: mercury golden imports SRI 75033
1962		cd: philips mercury 432 0032

EDOUARD LALO (1823-1892)

symphonie espagnole pour violon et orchestre
monte carlo
3-4 october 1972
monte carlo opera orchestra
amoyal, violin
lp: erato STU 70771

namouna, suite no 1
detroit
23-24 march 1958
detroit symphony
45: mercury XEP 9041
lp: mercury MG 50177/MG 50327/
MG 50334/MG 50339/MG 50376/
SR 90177/SR 90327/SR 90334/
SR 90339/SR 90376
lp: philips classical favourites GL 5833/
SGL 5833/832 869GY
cd: philips mercury 434 3892

rapsodie norvégienne
monte carlo
5october 1972
monte carlo opera orchestra
lp: erato STU 70771

le roi d'ys, overture
detroit
21 march 1958
detroit symphony
45: mercury XEP 9031
lp: mercury MG 50191/MG 50376/
SR 90191/SR 90376/AMS 16013
lp: mercury wing MGW 14071/SRW 18071
lp: philips classical favourites GL 5833/
SGL 5833/832 869GY
cd: philips mercury 434 3892

FRANZ LISZT (1811-1886)

mazeppa
monte carlo 2-4 june 1969   monte carlo opera orchestra   lp: concert hall SMSA 2648
lp: musidisc FC 416

orpheus
monte carlo 2-4 june 1969   monte carlo opera orchestra   lp: concert hall SMSA 2648
lp: musidisc FC 416

liszt **mephisto waltz no 2**

detroit
16 january
1959
	detroit
	symphony
		lp: mercury MG 50203/MG 50339/
		    MG 50359/SR 90203/SR 90339/
		    SR 90359/MMA 11093/AMS 16042
		lp: mercury wing MGW 14045/SRW 18087
		lp: philips 839 819GY
		cd: philips mercury 434 3362

monte carlo 2-4 june 1969	monte carlo opera orchestra	lp: concert hall SMSA 2648 lp: musidisc FC 416

les préludes

detroit 26-28 december 1953	detroit symphony	45: mercury XEP 9082 lp: mercury MG 50036/MLP 7523/ MMA 11080 lp: mercury wing MGW 14004/SRW 19004 lp: philips wing WL 1037
monte carlo 2-4 june 1959	monte carlo opera orchestra	lp: concert hall SMSA 2648 lp: musidisc FC 416

JULES MASSENET (1842-1912)

le cid, ballet music

monte carlo 22-24 may 1977	monte carlo opera orchestra	lp: concert hall SMSA 6507

phedre, overture

detroit 17 march 1962	detroit symphony	lp: mercury MG 50318/SR 90318 lp: mercury golden imports SRI 75078 cd: philips mercury 432 0142

FELIX MENDELSSOHN-BARTHOLDY (1809-1847)

symphony no 5 "reformation"
detroit	detroit	lp: mercury MG 50174/SR 90174/
21 march	symphony	MMA 11032/AMS 16022
1958		lp: mercury wing MGW 14067/SRW 18067
		lp: concert hall SMSA 2478
		cd: philips mercury 434 3962

a midsummer night's dream, suite: overture; scherzo; nocturne; wedding march
detroit	detroit	lp: mercury MG 50174/SR 90174/
21 march	symphony	MMA 11032/AMS 16022
1958		lp: mercury wing MGW 14067/SRW 18067
		cd: philips mercury 434 3962
		excerpts
		45: mercury XEP 9037/XEP 9095/
		SEX 15028/SEX 15035
		lp: mercury MG 50325/SR 90325/
		SR2-9131/SR2-9132

GIACOMO MEYERBEER (1791-1864)

marche du couronnement/le prophete
detroit	detroit	45: mercury XEP 9100
4 april	symphony	lp: mercury MG 50211/MG 50292/
1959		SR 90211/SR 90292/SR2-9131/
		MMA 11130/AMS 16077
		lp: philips classical favourites GL 5837/
		SGL 5837/837 871GY
		cd: philips mercury 434 3322

WOLFGANG AMADEUS MOZART (1756-1791)

symphony no 35 "haffner"
detroit	detroit	lp: mercury MG 50129/SR 90129/
21 october	symphony	MMA 11101/AMS 16052/49.006
1956		lp: mercury wing MGW 14046/SRW 18046
		lp: philips wing WL 1049
		lp: philips pergola 832 031PGY

piano concerto no 9 k271 "jeunehomme"
paris	lamoureux	78: grammophon 566 235-566 238
1946-1947	orchestra	78: vox (usa) 650
	g.casadesus, piano	lp: vox PL 8230/6500

violin concerto no 3 k216
paris	lamoureux	78: grammophon 566 230-566 232
27 november	orchestra	78: vox (usa) 642
1947	thibaud, violin	lp: vox PL 6420
		lp: columbia (japan) DXM 145
		cd: philips 420 8592

MODEST MUSSORGSKY (1839-1881)

night on bare mountain
paris	colonne	78: columbia LX 384
1945	orchestra	78: columbia (australia) LOX 251
		78: columbia (italy) GQX 10757
		78: columbia (belgium) BFX 14
		78: columbia (usa) 68305D

JACQUES OFFENBACH (1819-1880)

la belle hélene, overture

detroit 5 april 1959	detroit symphony	45: mercury XEP 9089/SEX 15030 lp: mercury MG 50215/MG 50359/ 　　SR 90215/SR 90359/MMA 11099/ 　　AMS 16045 lp: mercury wing MGW 14058/MGW 14086/ 　　SRW 18058/SRW 18086 lp: mercury golden imports SRI 75077 lp: philips DL 88028 cd: philips mercury 434 3322

les contes d'hoffmann, orchestral suite

detroit 5 april 1959	detroit symphony	lp: mercury MG 50215/MG 50377/ 　　SR 90215/SR 90377/MMA 11099/ 　　AMS 16045 lp: mercury wing MGW 14058/SRW 18058 lp: mercury golden imports SRI 75077 lp: philips classical favourites GL 5830/ 　　SGL 5830 cd: philips mercury 434 3322

orfée aux enfers, overture

detroit 5 april 1959	detroit symphony	45: mercury XEP 9111/SEX 15050 lp: mercury MG 50215/MG 50359/ 　　SR 90215/SR 90359/SR2-9139/ 　　MMA 11099/AMS 16045 lp: mercury wing MGW 14058/MGW 14086/ 　　SRW 18058/SRW 18086 lp: mercury golden imports SRI 75077 lp: philips 839 809GY lp: philips classical favourites GL 5839/ 　　SGL 5839/837 824GY cd: philips mercury 434 3322

PAUL PARAY (1886-1979)

symphony no 1
paris	orchestre	lp: carthagene 731 886
16 may	philharmonique	
1972	de l'ortf	

symphony no 2
paris	orchestre	lp: carthagene 731 889
27 november	national	
1968		

messe pour le cinquieme centenaire de la mort de jeanne d'arc
detroit	detroit	lp: mercury MG 50128/SR 90128
20 october	rackham	cd: philips mercury 432 7192
1956	chorus	
	yeend	
	bible	
	lloyd	
	kwei-sze	

paris	orchestral	lp: carthagene 731 891
14 november	national	
1973	and chorus	
	monteil	
	collard	
	lance	
	mars	

7 mélodies pour soprano et orchestre: le papillon; la plainte; infidelité; la derniere feuille; serment; le chevrier; il est d'étranges soirs
paris	orchestre	lp: carthagene 731 887
29 may	philharmonique	
1973	de l'ortf	
	monteil	

GABRIEL PIERNE (1863-1937)

cydalise et le chevre-pied, suite
paris	orchestre	lp: carthagene 731 886
16 may	philharmonique	
1972	de l'ortf	

marche des petits soldats de plomb
detroit	detroit	mercury unpublished
5 april	symphony	
1959		

SERGE PROKOFIEV (1891-1953)

piano concerto no 3
paris	orchestre	unpublished video recording
1963	national	
	janis, piano	

SERGEI RACHMANINOV (1873-1943)

symphony no 2
detroit	detroit	lp: mercury MG 50142/MG 50345/
18march	symphony	SR 90019/SR 90345/MMA 11052/
1957		AMS 16003
		lp: mercury wing MGW 14075/SRW 18075
		lp: philips fontana special SFL 14025
		cd: philips mercury 434 3682

MAURICE RAVEL (1875-1937)

piano concerto in g
paris 12-15 april 1965	orchestre national haas, piano	lp: dg LPM 18 988/SLPM 138 988
paris 3 march 1970	orchestre philharmonique de l'ortf lefébure, piano	cd: ina CD 55

piano concerto for the left hand
paris 12-15 april 1965	orchestre national haas, piano	lp: dg LPM 18 988/SLPM 138 988

alborada del gracioso
detroit 18 march 1962	detroit symphony	lp: mercury MG 50313/SR 90313 lp: mercury golden imports SRI 75033 cd: philips mercury 432 0032

boléro

detroit
24 march
1958
	detroit
	symphony
		lp: mercury MG 50020/MG 50373/
		    SR 90005/SR 90373/MLP 7509
		lp: mercury wing MGW 14031/SRW 18031
		lp: philips 6747 228/6870 577
		lp: philips wing WL 1020
		lp: philips fontana special SFL 14140/
		    700 455WGY
		cd: philips mercury 434 3062

ravel **daphnis et chloé, second suite**

detroit	detroit	lp: mercury MG 50281/SR 90281
11 march	symphony	lp: mercury golden imports SRI 75066
1961		cd: philips mercury 434 3062

ma mere l'oye

detroit	detroit	45: mercury XEP 9037
19 march	symphony	lp: mercury MG 50145/MG 50373/ SR 90005/SR 90373/MMA 11044
1957		lp: mercury golden imports SRI 75066
		lp: philips classical favourites GL 5834/ SGL 5834
		cd: philips mercury 434 3432

excerpts

lp: mercury MG 50532/SR 90532/ SR2-9132

pavane pour une infante défunte

detroit	detroit	lp: mercury MG 50313/MG 50373/ SR 90313/SR 90373
18 march	symphony	lp: mercury golden imports SRI 75033
1962		lp: philips classical favourites GL 5834/ SGL 5834
		cd: philips mercury 432 0032

ravel **rapsodie espagnole**
detroit	detroit	45: mercury XEP 9070
25 march	symphony	lp: mercury MG 50056
1955		lp: mercury wing MGW 14030/SRW 18030
detroit	detroit	lp: mercury MG 50313/SR 90313
18 march	symphony	lp: mercury golden imports SRI 75033
1962		cd: philips mercury 432 0032

le tombeau de couperin
detroit	detroit	45: mercury XEP 9096/SEX 15036
5 april	symphony	lp: mercury MG 50213/MG 50373/ SR 90213/SR 90373/MMA 11119/ AMS 16066
1959		lp: mercury wing MGW 14078/SRW 18078
		lp: mercury golden imports SRI 75100
		lp: philips classical favourites GL 5834/ SGL 5834
		cd: philips mercury 432 0032

la valse
detroit	detroit	lp: mercury MG 50029/MRL 2510/MLP 7509
7 december	symphony	lp: mercury wing MGW 14029/SRW 18029
1953		
detroit	detroit	lp: mercury MG 50313/SR 90313
18 march	symphony	lp: mercury golden imports SRI 75033
1962		lp: philips 6747 228/6870 577
		lp: philips fontana special SFL 14140/ 700 455WGY
		cd: philips mercury 432 0032
monte carlo	monte carlo	lp: concert hall SMSA 2563
october	opera orchestra	lp: musidisc FC 440
1969		

ravel **valses nobles et sentimentales**
detroit	detroit	lp: mercury MG 50213/MG 50373/
3 april	symphony	SR 90213/SR 90373/MMA 11119/
1959		AMS 16066
		lp: mercury wing MGW 14078/SRW 18078
		lp: mercury golden imports SRI 75066
		lp: philips 6747 228
		lp: philips classical favourites GL 5834/ SGL 5834
		cd: philips mercury 434 3062
		excerpts
		lp: mercury SR2-9127/SR2-9132

NIKOLAI RIMSKY-KORSAKOV (1844-1908)

symphony no 2 "antar"
detroit	detroit	lp: mercury MG 50028/MLP 7517/
7 december	symphony	MMA 11098
1953		lp: mercury wing MGW 14017/SRW 18017

capriccio espagnol
detroit	detroit	lp: mercury MG 50020/MLP 7509
february	symphony	lp: mercury wing MGW 14031/SRW 18031
1953		lp: philips wing WL 1020

russian easter festival overture
detroit	detroit	lp: mercury MG 50028/MLP 7517/
7 december	symphony	MMA 11098
1953		

GIOACCHINO ROSSINI (1792-1868)

guilleaume tell, overture

detroit	detroit	lp: mercury MG 50203/MG 50339/
16 january	symphony	MG 50359/SR 90203/SR 90339/
1959		SR 90359/SR2-9134/MMA 11093/
		AMS 16042

lp: mercury wing MGW 14045/MGW 14099/
SRW 18045/SRW 18099
lp: philips 6570 914
lp: philips classical favourites GL 5839/
SGL 5839/837 824GY
cd: philips mercury 434 3322

CLAUDE JOSEPH ROUGET DE LISLE (1760-1836)

la marseillaise

detroit	detroit	45: mercury XEP 9083/SEX 15025
5 april	symphony	lp: mercury MG 50211/MG 50374/
1959		MG 50504/SR 90211/SR 90374
		SR 90504/SR2-9131/MMA 11130/
		AMS 16077

cd: philips mercury 434 3322

ALBERT ROUSSEL (1869-1937)

le festin de l'araignée, suite

detroit	detroit	lp: mercury MG 50035/MRL 2500/
26-28	symphony	MLP 7519/MMA 11096
december		lp: mercury wing MGW 14036/SRW 18036
1953		

suite in f

detroit	detroit	lp: mercury MG 50145/MMA 11044
19 march	symphony	lp: mercury golden imports SRI 75100
1957		cd: philips mercury 434 3032

CAMILLE SAINT-SAENS (1835-1921)

symphony no 3 "organ"
detroit	detroit	lp: mercury MG 50167/MG 50331/
12 october	symphony	SR 90012/SR 90331/MMA 11039/
1957		AMS 16004
		lp: mercury golden imports SRI 75003
		lp: philips grandioso 894 022ZKY
		cd: philips mercury 432 7192

piano concerto no 2
paris	colonne	78: pathé PDT 167-169
1939	orchestra	
	darré, piano	

danse macabre
detroit	detroit	45: mercury XEP 9081/SEX 15024
16 january	symphony	lp: mercury MG 50203/MG 50339/
1959		MG 50359/SR 90203/SR 90339/
		SR 90359/MMA 11093/AMS 16042
		lp: mercury wing MGW 14045/SRW 18045
		lp: philips 6870 577
		lp: philips fontana special SFL 14140/
		700 455WGY
		cd: philips mercury 434 3362
monte carlo	monte carlo	lp: concert hall SMSA 6507
22-24	opera orchestra	
may		
1977		

marche héroique
detroit	detroit	45: mercury XEP 9109
5 april	symphony	lp: mercury MG 50211/MG 50325/
1958		MG 50374/SR 90211/SR 90325/
		SR 90374/MMA 11130/AMS 16077
		cd: mercury philips 434 3322

saint-saens **marche militaire francaise/suite algérienne**

detroit	detroit	45: mercury XEP 9083/SEX 15025
4 april	symphony	lp: mercury MG 50211/MG 50292/
1959		SR 90211/SR 90292/MMA 11130/
		AMS 16077
		cd: philips mercury 434 3322

le rouet d'omphale

monte carlo	monte carlo	lp: concert hall SMSA 6507
22-24	opera orchestra	
may		
1977		

bacchanale/samson et dalila

detroit	detroit	lp: mercury MG 50318/MG 50327/
11march	symphony	SR 90318/SR 90327/SR2-9130
1961		lp: mercury golden imports SRI 75078
		lp: philips 6747 228
		cd: mercury philips 434 0142

FLORENT SCHMITT (1865-1958)

la tragédie de salomé

detroit	detroit	lp: mercury MG 50177/MG 50327/
23 march	symphony	MG 50334/MG 50339/MG 50376/
1958		SR 90012/SR 90327/SR 90334/
		SR 90339/SR 90376
		cd: philips mercury 434 3362

ROBERT SCHUMANN (1810-1856)

symphony no 1 "spring"

detroit	detroit	mercury unpublished
1958	symphony	

detroit	detroit	lp: mercury MG 50198/MG 50330/
16-18	symphony	SR 90198/SR 90330/MMA 11070/
january		AMS 16017
1959		lp: mercury wing MGW 14083/SRW 18083
		cd: philips mercury 462 9552

symphony no 2

detroit	detroit	lp: mercury MG 50102/SR 90102/
2 december	symphony	MRL 2519/MMA 11065
1955		lp: mercury wing MGW 14061/SRW 18061
		lp: concert hall M 207
		cd: philips mercury 462 9552

symphony no 3 "rhenish"

detroit	detroit	lp: mercury MG 50133/MG 50330/
9 november	symphony	SR 90133/SR 90330/MMA 11088/
1956		AMS 16035
		lp: mercury wing MGW 14059/SRW 18059
		cd: philips mercury 462 9552

schumann **symphony no 4**

detroit	detroit	lp: mercury MG 50036/MLP 7523/
26-28	symphony	MMA 11080
december		lp: mercury wing MGW 14004/SRW 18004
1953		lp: philips wing WL 1037
		lp: philips fontana special 700 061WGY
		cd: philips mercury 462 9552

piano concerto

paris	orchestre	lp: ina CD 55
18-19	philharmonique	
march	de l'ortf	
1970	lefébure, piano	

manfred overture

detroit	detroit	mercury unpublished
1958	symphony	

detroit	detroit	lp: mercury MG 50198/MG 50323/
16-18	symphony	SR 90198/SR 90323/MMA 11070/
january		AMS 16017
1959		cd: philips mercury 462 9552

JEAN SIBELIUS (1865-1957)

symphony no 2
detroit	detroit	lp: mercury MG 50204/SR 90204/
17 january	symphony	MMA 11109/AMS 16061
1959		lp: mercury wing MGW 14057/SRW 18057
		cd: philips mercury 434 3172

first movement
lp: mercury SR2-9128

RICHARD STRAUSS (1864-1949)

dance of the seven veils/salome
detroit	detroit	lp: mercury MG 50177/MG 50327/
23 march	symphony	MG 50339/MG 50376/SR 90177/
1958		SR 90327/SR 90339/SR 90376/
		SR2-9130
		lp: mercury wing MGW 14045/SRW 18045
		lp: mercury golden imports SRI 75015
		lp: philips classical favourites GL 5831/
		SGL 5831

till eulenspiegels lustige streiche
amsterdam	concertgebouw	cd: q-disc Q 97017
18 january	orchestra	
1940		

FRANZ VON SUPPE (1819-1895)

boccaccio, overture
detroit	detroit	45: mercury XEP 9105/SEX 15044
29 november	symphony	lp: mercury MG 50269/SR 90269
1959		lp: mercury wing MGW 14094/SRW 18094
		lp: mercury golden imports SRI 75091
		lp: philips 839 308GY
		lp: philips fontana 6531 012
		lp: philips grandioso 894 081ZKY
		cd: philips mercury 434 3092

the beautiful galathea, overture
detroit	detroit	lp: mercury MG 50269/SR 90269
29 november	symphony	lp: mercury wing MGW 14094/SRW 18094
1959		lp: mercury golden imports SRI 75091
		lp: philips 839 308GY
		lp: philips fontana 6531 012
		lp: philips grandioso 894 081ZKY
		cd: philips mercury 434 3092

light cavalry, overture
detroit	detroit	45: mercury XEP 9105/SEX 15044
29 november	symphony	lp: mercury MG 50269/SR 90269
1959		lp: mercury golden imports SRI 75091
		lp: philips DL 88028/839 308GY
		lp: philips fontana 6531 012
		lp: philips grandioso 894 081ZKY
		cd: philips mercury 434 3092

suppé morning, noon and night in vienna, overture
detroit	detroit	45: mercury XEP 9098/SEX 15038
29 november	symphony	lp: mercury MG 50269/SR 90269
1959		lp: mercury wing MGW 14094/SRW 18094
		lp: mercury golden imports SRI 75091
		lp: philips 839 308GY
		lp: philips fontana 6531 012
		lp: philips grandioso 894 081ZKY
		cd: philips mercury 434 3092

pique dame, overture
detroit	detroit	45: mercury XEP 9098/SEX 15038
29 november	symphony	lp: mercury MG 50269/SR 90269
1959		lp: mercury wing MGW 14094/SRW 18094
		lp: mercury golden imports SRI 75091
		lp: philips 839 308GY
		lp: philips fontana 6531 012
		lp: philips grandioso 894 081ZKY
		cd: philips mercury 434 3092

poet and peasant, overture
detroit	detroit	45: mercury XEP 9087/SEX 15028
29 november	symphony	lp: mercury MG 50269/SR 90269/SR2-9134
1959		lp: mercury wing MGW 14094/SRW 18094
		lp: mercury golden imports SRI 75091
		lp: philips 839 308GY/SDAL 502
		lp: philips classical favourites GL 5839/ SGL 5839/837 824GY
		lp: philips fontana 6531 012
		lp: philips grandioso 894 081ZKY
		cd: philips mercury 434 3092

FRENCH OPERA HIGHLIGHTS

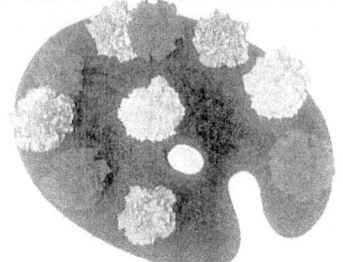

GOUNOD Faust: Ballet Music and Waltz
SAINT-SAËNS Samson and Delilah: Bacchanale
BIZET Carmen: Danse Bohème
BERLIOZ The Trojans: Royal Hunt and Storm
MASSENET Phèdre: Overture
THOMAS Mignon: Gavotte
HEROLD Zampa: Overture
AUBER The Crown Diamonds: Overture

PAUL PARAY conducting the DETROIT SYMPHONY ORCHESTRA

PIOTR TCHAIKOVSKY (1840-1893)

violin concerto
boston	boston	lp: discocorp RR 453
30 november	symphony	
1945	elman, violin	

AMBROISE THOMAS (1811-1896)

mignon, overture
detroit detroit lp: mignon MG 50247/MG 50324./
19 november symphony MG 50377/SR 90247/SR 90324/
1960   SR 90377/SR2-9130
   lp: mercury golden imports SRI 75077
   lp: philips DL 88028
   cd: philips mercury 434 3212

gavotte/mignon
detroit detroit lp: mercury MG 50318/SR 90318
17 march symphony cd: philips mercury 432 0142
1962

raymonda, overture
detroit detroit lp: mercury MG 50247/MG 50324/
19 november symphony MG 50377/SR 90247/SR 90324/
1960   SR 90377/SR2-9134
   lp: philips classical favourites GL 5830/
   SGL 5830
   cd: philips mercury 434 3212

RICHARD WAGNER (1813-1883)

der fliegende holländer, overture
detroit	detroit	lp: mercury MG 50044/MRL 2531
26 november	symphony	lp: mercury wing MGW 14019/SRW 18019
1954		lp: philips wing WL 1013

detroit	detroit	45: mercury XEP 9095/SEX 15035
20 february	symphony	lp: mercury MG 50232/MG 50333/
1960		SR 90232/SR 90333/SR2-9134
		cd: philips mercury 434 3832

lohengrin, prelude
detroit	detroit	45: mercury XEP 9055/EP1-5045
february	symphony	lp: mercury MG 50021/MRL 2513/
1953		MLP 7504
		lp: mercury wing MGW 14015/SRW 18015
		lp: philips wing WL 1010

lohengrin, act 3 prelude
detroit	detroit	lp: mercury MG 50021/MRL 2513/
february	symphony	MLP 7504
1953		lp: mercury wing MGW 14015/SRW 18015
		lp: philips wing WL 1010

götterdämmerung, dawn and siegfried's rhine journey
detroit	detroit	lp: mercury MG 50107/MG 50333/
23-24	symphony	SR 90107/SR 90333/SR2-9130/
march		MMA 11056/AMS 16049
1956		lp: mercury wing MGW 14054/SRW 18054
		lp: philips wing WL 1085
		lp: philips classical favourites GL 5821/
		SGL 5821
		cd: philips mercury 434 3832

wagner die meistersinger von nürnberg, overture
detroit	detroit	lp: mercury MG 50021/MRL 2513/
february	symphony	MLP 7504
1953		lp: mercury wing MGW 14015/SRW 18015
		lp: philips wing WL 1010

die meistersinger von nürnberg, suite: act 3 prelude; dance of the apprentices; entry of the masters
detroit	detroit	45: mercury XEP 9101/SEX 15040
20 february	symphony	lp: mercury MG 50232/MG 50333/
1960		SR 90232/SR 90333
		lp: philips classical favourites GL 5821/ SGL 5821
		cd: philips mercury 434 3832

parsifal, prelude
detroit	detroit	lp: mercury MG 50107/SR 90107/
23-24	symphony	MMA 11056/AMS 16049
march		lp: mercury wing MGW 14054/SRW 18054
1956		lp: philips wing WL 1085

parsifal, karfreitagszauber
detroit	detroit	lp: mercury MG 50044/MRL 2531
26 november	symphony	lp: mercury wing MGW 14019/SRW 18019
1954		lp: philips wing WL 1013

wagner rienzi, overture
detroit
20 february
1960

detroit
symphony

lp: mercury MG 50232/MG 50333/
SR 90232/SR 90333
cd: philips mercury 434 3832

siegfried idyll
detroit
23-24
march
1956

detroit
symphony

45: mercury XEP 9068/SEX 15016
lp: mercury MG 50107/SR 90107
MMA 11056/AMS 16049
lp: mercury wing MGW 14054/SRW 18054
lp: philips wing WL 1085
cd: philips mercury 434 3832

siegfried, forest murmurs
detroit
26 november
1954

detroit
symphony

45: mercury XEP 9085
lp: mercury MG 50044/MRL 2531
lp: mercury wing MGW 14019/SRW 18019
lp: philips wing WL 1013

tannhäuser, overture
detroit
february
1953

detroit
symphony

lp: mercury MG 50021/MRL 2513/
MLP 7504
lp: mercury wing MGW 14015/SRW 18015
lp: philips wing WL 1010

tristan und isolde, prelude
detroit
26 november
1954

detroit
symphony

mercury unpublished

wagner tristan und isolde, act 3 prelude

detroit	detroit	45: mercury XEP 9085
23-24	symphony	lp: mercury MG 50107/MG 50333/
march		SR 90107/SR 90333/MMA 11056/
1956		AMS 16049
		lp: mercury wing MGW 14054/SRW 18054
		lp: philips wing WL 1085
		lp: philips fontana special SFL 14051
		lp: philips classical favourites GL 5821/
		SGL 5821
		cd: philips mercury 434 3832

tristan und isolde, prelude and liebestod

detroit	detroit	lp: mercury MG 50044/MRL 2531
25 march	symphony	lp: mercury wing MGW 14019/SRW 18019
1955		lp: mercury wing WL 1013
paris	orchestre	lp: carthagene 731 888
27 november	national	
1968		

146

wagner die walküre, ride of the valkyries
detroit	detroit	45: mercury XEP 9055/MEP 14510/
february	symphony	EP1-5045
1953		lp: mercury MG 50021/MRL 2513/
		MLP 7504
		lp: mercury wing MGW 14015/SRW 18015
		lp: philips wing WL 1010

die walküre, wotan's farewell and magic fire music
detroit	detroit	lp: mercury MG 50232/MG 50333/
20 february	symphony	SR 90232/SR 90333
1960		cd: philips mercury 434 3832

CARL MARIA VON WEBER (1786-1826)

aufforderung zum tanz, arranged by berlioz
detroit	detroit	lp: mercury MG 50203/MG 50339/
16 january	symphony	MG 50359/SR 90203/SR 90339/
1959		SR 90359/MMA 11093/AMS 16042
		lp: mercury wing MGW 14045/SRW 18045
		cd: philips mercury 434 3362

pierre monteux
1875-1964

HENDRIK ANDRIESSEN (1892-1981)

organ concerto
amsterdam	concerrgebouw	cd: q-disc Q 97017
1 november	orchestra	
1950	andriessen, organ	

JOHANN SEBASTIAN BACH (1685-1750)

orchestral suite no 2
london	london	lp: decca LXT 6112/SXL 6112
3-8	symphony	lp: london (usa) CM 9400/CS 6400/
november	c.monteux,	STS 15493
1963	flute	

concerto for 2 violins bwv1043
paris	orchestre	78: hmv DB 1718-1719
4 june	symphonique	78: victor M 932
1932	de paris	lp: hmv COLH 77
	menuhin and	lp: hmv (france) FJLP 5018
	enesco, violins	lp: victor LCT 1120/LVT 1006
		cd: emi CDH 567 2012
		cd: dante LYS 374

passacaglia and fugue in c minor bwv582, arranged by respighi
san francisco	san francisco	78: hmv DB 21053-21054
19 april	symphony	78: victor M 1340
1949		45: victor WDM 1340
		lp: victor LCT 1039/LM 1799/LM 149
		cd: rca/bmg 09026 618922

sinfonia/weihnachtsoratorium
san francisco	san francisco	78: hmv DB 21054
19 april	symphony	78: victor M 1340
1949		45: victor WDM 1340

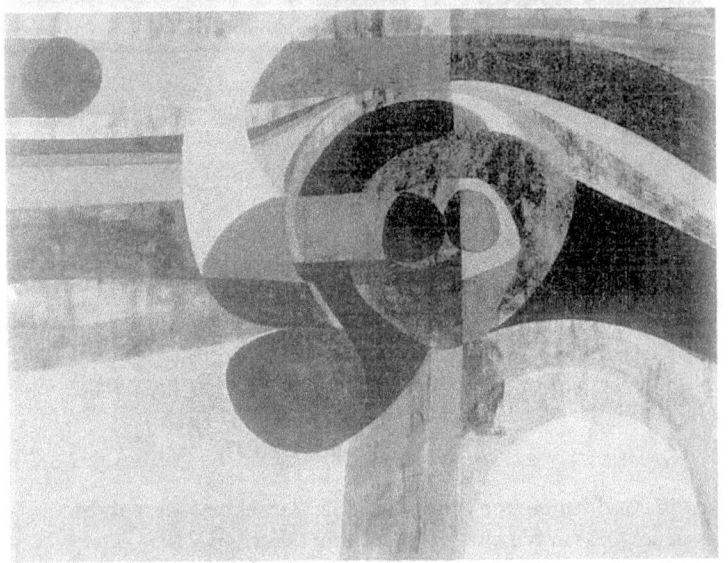

LUDWIG VAN BEETHOVEN (1770-1827)

symphony no 1
vienna 20-24 april 1960	vienna philharmonic	lp: victor LM 2491/LSC 2491/RB 16256/ SB 2127/VIC 1148/VICS 1148 lp: decca ECM 638/ECS 638 lp: london (usa) STS 15238 cd: decca 433 4222/440 6272/443 4792

symphony no 2
san francisco 19 april 1949	san francisco symphony	78: victor M 1325 45: victor WDM 1325 lp: hmv (france) FALP 114 lp: hmv (italy) QALP 114 lp: victor LM 1024 lp: victor (france) 43357
walthamstow 9-10 may 1960	london symphony	lp: victor VIC 1170/VICS 1170 lp: london (usa) STS 15518 cd: decca 443 7492
hamburg october 1960	ndr orchestra	lp: concert hall SMSA 2332 cd: fnac 642 302 cd: emi CZS 575 4742 cd: scribendum SC 013

beethoven **symphony no 3 "eroica"**

vienna 2-3 december 1957	vienna philharmonic	lp: victor VIC 1036/VICS 1036 lp: decca SPA 113 lp: london (usa) STS 15518 cd: decca 433 4222/440 6272
london 12 november 1960	royal philharmonic	cd: bbc legends BBCL 41122

amsterdam
1-3
july
1962
	concertgebouw
	orchestra
		lp: philips A02247L/A02393L/
		    835 132AY/6768 339/6856 003
		cd: philips 420 8532/442 5442
		rehearsal extracts
		lp: philips A02455-02456L/
		    835 325-835 326AY
		lp: philips classical favourites GL 5788

symphony no 4

san francisco 7 april 1952	san francisco symphony	45: victor WDM 1714 lp: victor LM 1714 cd: rca/bmg 09026 618922
london 15-16 october 1959	london symphony	lp: victor VIC 1102/VICS 1102 lp: london (usa) STS 15394 cd: decca 443 7492
hamburg october 1960	ndr orchestra	lp: concert hall SMSA 2332 cd: fnac 642 302 cd: scribendum SC 013

beethoven **symphony no 5**
san francisco	san francisco	cd: music and arts CD 978
16 february	symphony	*certain sections of the recording are replaced by a*
1947		*performance dated 10 december 1950*

london	london	lp: london (usa) STS 15519
25-27	symphony	cd: decca 443 7492
may		
1961		

symphony no 6 "pastoral"
vienna	vienna	lp: victor LM 2316/VICS 2316/RB 16181/
28-29	philharmonic	SB 2065/VIC 1070/VICS 1070
october		lp: decca SPA 113
1958		lp: london (usa) STS 15161
		cd: decca 433 4222/440 6272

symphony no 7
new york	nbc symphony	lp: longanesi GCL 28
15 november		
1953		

paris	orchestre	cd: rappel 2
9 june	national	
1955		

london	london	lp: victor VIC 1061/VICS 1061
25-27	symphony	lp: decca SPA 586
may		lp: london (usa) STS 15520
1961		cd: decca 443 7492

beethoven **symphony no 8**

san francisco 28 february 1950	san francisco symphony	78: victor M 1450 45: victor WDM 1450 lp: victor LCT 1039/LM 1799/LM 43 lp: victor (france) 43357 cd: rca/bmg 09026 618922
vienna 15-22 april 1959	vienna philharmonic	lp: victor LM 2491/LSC 2491/RB 16256/ SB 2127/VIC 1148/VICS 1148 lp: decca ECM 638/ECS 638 lp: london (usa) STS 15238 cd: decca 433 4222/440 6372

chicago
1 january
1960
1961
	chicago
	symphony
		vhs video: video artists international
		   VAI 69604
		dvd video: video artists international
		   VAIDVD 4226

symphony no 9 "**choral**"

walthamstow
11-13
june
1962
	london
	symphony
	bach choir
	söderström
	resnik
	vickers
	ward
		lp: westminster XWN 2234/WST 234/
		   WGS 8364/PWN 330
		lp: westminster heliodor 478 642
		lp: westminster emi 1C045 90337
		lp: world records T 415-416/ST 415-416
		lp: véga MT 10196
		lp: columbia (japan) OS 8006-8007
		cd: millenium classics MCAD2-9806/
		   MCD 80090
		cd: dg westminster 471 2162

recording completed on 18 june 1962; certain lp editions may have contained rehearsal extracts

beethoven **piano concerto no 5 "emperor"**
vienna	vienna	lp: discocorp RR 558
16 october	symphony	
1958	badura-skoda,	
	piano	

egmont, overture
san francisco	san francisco	cd: music and arts CD 978
23 december	symphony	
1951		

london	london	lp: london (usa) STS 15519
25-27	symphony	cd: decca 443 7492
may		
1961		

fidelio, overture
san francisco	san francisco	cd: music and arts CD 978
16 january	symphony	
1944		

walthamstow	london	lp: victor VIC 1170/VICS 1170
9-10	symphony	lp: london (usa) STS 15518
may		
1960		

beethoven **die geschöpfe des prometheus, overture**

san francisco 17 december 1944	san francisco symphony	cd: music and arts CD 978

hamburg 6-14 february 1964	ndr orchestra	45: concert hall M 503 lp: concert hall SMSA 2761

die geschöpfe des prometheus, adagio from the ballet music

hamburg 6-14 february 1964	ndr orchestra	45: concert hall M 503 lp: concert hall SMSA 2761 cd: scribendum SC 013

könig stephan, overture

walthamstow 9-10 may 1960	london symphony	lp: victor VIC 1170/VICS 1170 lp: london (usa) STS 15518 cd: decca 443 7492

leonore no 3, overture

san francisco 30 march 1952	san francisco symphony	cd: music and arts CD 978

london 15-16 october 1959	london symphony	decca/victor unpublished

beethoven **die ruinen von athen, overture**
san francisco	san francisco	45: victor WDM 1637
19 april	symphony	45: victor (italy) B72R 0011
1949		cd: rca/bmg 09026 618922

die weihe des hauses, overture
san francisco	san francisco	cd: music and arts CD 978
4 december	symphony	
1949		
amsterdam	concertgebouw	cd: audophile APL 100 559
12 october	orchestra	
1950		

HECTOR BERLIOZ (1803-1869)

symphonie fantastique

paris 20-28 january 1930	orchestre symphonique de paris	78: hmv D 2044-2049 78: hmv (france) W 1100-1105 78: victor M 111 cd: pearl GEMMCD 9329/GEMMCD 9016 cd: dante LYS 374 cd: music and arts CD 762 cd: cascavelle 210 912
san francisco 27-28 february 1945	san francisco symphony	78: hmv DB 6670-6675/DB 9342-9347 auto 78: victor M 994 45: victor WDM 994 cd: archipel ARPCD 0146
amsterdam 20 may 1948	concertgebouw orchestra	cd: tahra TAH 178
san francisco 27 february 1950	san francisco symphony	lp: hmv ALP 1137 lp: hmv (france) FALP 118 lp: hmv (italy) QALP 118 lp: victor LM 1131 lp: victor (france) 43559 cd: victor (japan) BVCC 37321
vienna 20-24 october 1958	vienna philharmonic	lp: victor LM 2362/LSC 2362/ VIC 1031/VICS 1031 cd: polygram (japan) KICC 8413
hamburg 6-14 february 1964	ndr orchestra	lp: concert hall SMSA 2357 lp: musidisc FC 404 cd: scribendum SC 013

berlioz **harold en italie**

amsterdam	concertgebouw	lp: past masters PM 37
11 november	orchestra	cd: audiophile APL 101 558
1963	boon, viola	*audiophile edition is dated 24 november 1963*

benvenuto cellini, overture

paris	orchestre	78: hmv D 2060-2061
30 january	symphonique	78: hmv (france) W 1141-1142
1930	de paris	78: victor 11.140-11.141
		cd: pearl GEMMCD 9012
		cd: dante LYS 368
		cd: music and arts CD 762
amsterdam	concertgebouw	cd: q-disc Q 97017
12 october	orchestra	
1938		
san francisco	san francisco	victor unpublished
22 december	symphony	
1947		
san francisco	san francisco	45: victor ERB 5
6 april	symphony	lp: victor LVT 1039/LM 1799
1952		lp: victor (italy) A12R 0158
		lp: victor (france) 43559

le carnaval romain, overture

san francisco	san francisco	cd: music and arts CD 978
8 december	symphony	
1946		
chicago	chicago	vhs video: video artists international
1 january	symphony	VAI 69604
1961		dvd video: video artists international
		VAIDVD 4226

berlioz le corsaire, overture
san francisco   san francisco   cd: music and arts CD 978
9 march   symphony
1952

la damnation de faust
london	london	lp: discocorp RR 539
8 march	symphony	cd: music and arts CD 928/CD 4928
1962	orchestra	cd: bbc legends BBCL 40062
	and chorus	
	crespin	
	turp	
	roux	

menuet des follets; ballet des sylphes/la damnation de faust
san francisco   san francisco   cd: music and arts CD 978
26 november   symphony
1948

marche hongroise/la damnation de faust
san francisco   san francisco   cd: music and arts CD 978
26 november   symphony
1948

san francisco	san francisco	45: victor WDM 1618/ERB 5
3 april	symphony	45: hmv (france) 7RF 278
1951		lp: rca camden CAL 385/CDN 1005
		cd: rca/bmg 09026 618942

london   london   cd: bbc legends BBCL 41122
15 december   symphony
1961

la fuite en égypte/l'enfance du christ
san francisco	san francisco	cd: music and arts CD 978
21 december	symphony	*sections of the recording are taken from another*
1947		*performance dated 28 march 1948*

berlioz **roméo et juliette**
walthamstow	london	lp: westminster XWN 2233/WST 233
18-21	symphony	cd: millenium classics MCAD2-9805
june	orchestra	cd: dg westminster 471 2422
1962	and chorus	
	resnik	
	turp	
	ward	

roméo et juliette, scenes: combat; tumult; roméo seul; fete chez capulet; scene d'amour
san francisco	san francisco	cd: music and arts CD 978
26 november	symphony	
1948		

les troyens a carthage, prelude
paris	orchestre	78: hmv D 2061
31 january	symphonique	78: hmv (france) W 1142
1930	de paris	78: victor 11-141
		cd: pearl GEMMCD 9016
san francisco	san francisco	cd: rca/bmg 09026 618942
27 january	symphony	*unpublished victor 78rpm recording*
1945		
san francisco	san francisco	cd: music and arts CD 978
18 november	symphony	
1945		

absence/les nuits d'été
san francisco	san francisco	cd: eklipse EKRCD 55
5 march	symphony	
1950	tourel	

ALEXANDER BORODIN (1833-1887)

polovtsian dances/prince igor
san francisco 23 december 1951	san francisco symphony	cd: music and arts CD 978
hamburg 6-14 february 1964	ndr orchestra	45: concert hall M 505 lp: concert hall SMSA 2761/SMSA 5220 lp: turnabout TV 34668 cd: scribendum SC 013

JOHANNES BRAHMS (1833-1897)

symphony no 1
amsterdam   concertgebouw   cd: tahra TAH 177
20 november   orchestra
1963

symphony no 1, second movement
san francisco   san francisco   cd: music and arts CD 978
23 december   symphony
1951

brahms **symphony no 2**

san francisco 19 march 1945	san francisco symphony	78: victor M 1065 45: victor WDM 1065 cd: andante 1973
san francisco 4 april 1951	san francisco symphony	lp: victor LM 1173 cd: rca/bmg 09026 618912/74321 845882
vienna 13-15 april 1959	vienna philharmonic	lp: victor LM 6411/LSC 6411/RB 16241/ SB 2110/VIC 1055/VICS 1055 lp: decca ECM 596/ECS 596 lp: london (usa) STS 15192
walthamstow 28 november- 1 december 1962	london symphony	lp: philips AL 3435/A02287L/ SAL 3435/835 167AY/6768 339 lp: philips (usa) 500 035/900 035 cd: philips 442 5442/442 5472

symphony no 3

amsterdam 30 october 1960	concertgebouw orchestra	cd: tahra TAH 176
manchester 21 november 1962	bbc northern symphony	cd: bbc legends BBCL 40582

brahms **piano concerto no 1**
london	london	lp: decca LXT 5546/SXL 2172
24-25	symphony	lp: london (usa) CM 9030/CS 6151/
march	katchen, piano	STS 15209
1959		lp: contour classics CC 7587
		cd: decca 440 6122

violin concerto
amsterdam	concertgebouw	cd: tahra TAH 176
12 october	orchestra	cd: audiophile classics APL 101 559
1950	milstein, violin	

new york	new york	cd: one eleven 50400
22 january	philharmonic	
1956	milstein, violin	

london	london	lp: victor LM 2281/LSC 2281/RB 16168/
18-20	symphony	SB 2049/VIC 1028/VICS 1028
june	szeryng, violin	AGL1-5216
1958		cd: rca/bmg 74321 845882

double concerto
milan	rai milano	cd: stradivarius STR 10013
12 april	orchestra	
1964	grumiaux, violin	
	janigro, cello	

haydn variations
london	london	lp: victor LM 2418/LSC 2418/RB 16281/
8-9	symphony	SB 2108
december		lp: london (usa) STS 15188
1958		cd: decca 452 3032

brahms **academic festival overture**

walthamstow	london	lp: philips AL 3435/A02287L/
28 november-	symphony	SAL 3435/835 167AY/6768 339
1 december		lp: philips (usa) 500 035/900 035
1962		cd: philips 442 5442/442 5472

tragic overture

san francisco	san francisco	cd: music and arts CD 978
20 february	symphony	
1949		

amsterdam	concertgebouw	cd: tahra TAH 177
14 may	orchestra	
1962		

waltzes op 39 nos 1, 2, 11, 14 and 15, arranged by hertz

san francisco	san francisco	cd: music and arts CD 978
27 march	symphony	
1949		

alto rhapsody

san francisco	san francisco	78: victor M 1111/SP 13
3 march	symphony	lp: victor (italy) A12R 0085
1945	and mens	lp: hmv ALP 1138
	chorus	
	anderson	

song of destiny

san francisco	san francisco	45: victor WDM 1637
16 april	symphony	lp: victor LM 149
1949	stanford	lp: victor (italy) B72R 0011-0012
	university	cd: rca/bmg 09026 618912
	chorus	

MAX BRUCH (1838-1920)

violin concerto no 1

san francisco	san francisco	78: victor M 1023
27 january	symphony	cd: biddulph LAB 129
1945	menuhin,	
	violin	

EMMANUEL CHABRIER (1841-1894)

fete polonaise/le roi malgré lui

paris	orchestre	78: hmv (france) W 0796
29 january	symphonique	cd: pearl GEMMCD 9016
1930	de paris	cd: dante LYS 368
		cd: cascavelle 210 912
san francisco	san francisco	78: victor 12-0978
22 december	symphony	45: victor 49-0517
1947		cd: rca/bmg 09026 618992

ERNEST CHAUSSON (1855-1899)

symphony in b flat
san francisco	san francisco	45: victor WDM 1582
20 february	symphony	lp: victor LM 1181
1950		lp: victor (italy) A12R 0021
		lp: victor (france) 43557
		lp: hmv (france) FALP 227
		cd: rca/bmg 09026 618992
		cd: cascavelle 210 912

poeme pour violon et orchestre
san francisco	san francisco	cd: testament SBT 1216
17 december	symphony	*unpublished victor 78rpm recording*
1945	heifetz, violin	

poeme de l'amour et de la mer
new york	rca victor	lp: victor LVT 1038/LM 1793
9 december	orchestra	lp: victor (italy) A12R 0158
1952	swarthout	lp: victor (france) A 630227/43557
		lp: hmv ALP 1269
		cd: rca/bmg 09026 618992
		cd: archipel ARPCD 0146

LUIGI CHERUBINI (1760-1842)

anacréon, overture
london	royal	cd: bbc legends BBCL 41122
25 january	philharmonic	
1960		

PIERO COPPOLA (1888-1971)

interlude dramatique
paris	orchestre	78: hmv (france) W 1106
3 february	symphonique	cd: pearl GEMMCD 9016
1930	de paris	cd: dante LYS 374

CLAUDE DEBUSSY (1862-1918)

la mer

amsterdam 12 october 1939	concergebouw orchestra	cd: q-disc Q 97017
boston 19 july 1954	boston symphony	lp: victor LM 1939 lp: victor (france) 43366 cd: victor (japan) BVCC 3732 *excerpts* cd: rca/bmg 09026 685242

trois nocturnes

boston 15august 1955	boston symphony berkshire festival chorus	lp: victor LM 1939/VIC 1027/VICS 1027 lp: victor (france) 43366 cd: emi CZS 575 4742 *nuages and fetes only* lp: victor RB 6533

nuages et fetes/trois nocturnes

london 11-13 december 1961	london symphony	45: decca CEP 5510/SEC 5510 lp: decca LXT 5677/SXL 2312 lp: london (usa) CM 9317/CS 6248/ STS 15356

prélude a l'apres-midi d'un faune

amsterdam 12 october 1950	concertgebouw orchestra	cd: audiophile APL 101 559
london 11-13 december 1961	london symphony	lp: decca LXT 5677/SXL 2312 lp: london (usa) CM 9317/CS 6248/ STS 15356

debussy l'enfant prodigue, excerpt (l'année en vain)
san francisco	san francisco	cd: cambria CD 1111
13 april	symphony	
1942	warenskjold	

gigues/images pour orchestra
san francisco	san francisco	78: hmv DB 6182-6183
2 march	symphony	78: victor M 954
1942		lp: victor (italy) A72R 0019
		lp: rca camden CAL 161
		cd: cascavelle 210 912
san francisco	san francisco	78: hmv (france) DB 11139
3 april	symphony	45: victor WDM 1618/WEPR 12
1951		lp: victor LVT 1036/LM 1197
		lp: hmv (france) FALP 174
paris	orchestre	lp: discocorp RR 313
3 may	national	
1956		
walthamstow	london	lp: philips AL 3459/A02323L/
18-21	symphony	SAL 3459/835 205AY/6768 339
may		lp: philips (usa) 500 058/900 058
1963		cd: philips 420 3922/442 5442/442 5952

ibéria/images pour orchestre

san francisco 3 april 1951	san francisco symphony	45: victor WDM 1618 lp: victor LVT 1036/LM 1197 lp: hmv (france) FALP 174
paris 3 may 1956	orchestre national	lp: discocorp RR 313
london 18 october 1961	bbc symphony	cd: bbc legends BBCL 40962
walthamstow 18-21 may 1963	london symphony	lp: philips AL 3459/A02323L/ SAL 3459/835 205AY/6768 339 lp: philips (usa) 500 058/900 058 cd: philips 420 3922/442 5442/442 5952

rondes de printemps/images pour orchestre

san francisco 2 march 1942	san francisco symphony	78: hmv DB 6182-6183 78: victor M 954 lp: victor (italy) A72R 0019 lp: rca camden CAL 161 cd: cascavelle 210 912
san francisco 3 april 1951	san francisco symphony	45: victor WDM 1618/WEPR 12 lp: victor LVT 1036/LM 1197 lp: hmv (france) FALP 174 lp: rca camden CAL 336
walthamstow 18-21 may 1963	london symphony	lp: philips AL 3459/A02323L/ SAL 3459/835 105AY/6768 339 lp: philips (usa) 500 058/900 058 cd: philips 420 3922/442 5442/442 5952

debussy **jeux**
paris   orchestre   cd: rappel CD 2
9 june   national
1955

le martyre de san sébastien
boston   boston   lp: discocorp RR 313
10 january   symphony
1958

walthamstow   london   lp: philips AL 3459/A02323L/
18-21   symphony   SAL 3459/835 205AY/6768 339
may   lp: philips (usa) 500 058/900 058
1963   cd: philips 420 3922/442 5442/442 5952

pelléas et mélisande, orchestral suite from the opera
boston   boston   lp: discocorp RR 313
18 february   symphony
1957

sarabande/pour le piano, arranged by ravel
san francisco   san francisco 78: victor M 1143
3 april   symphony   lp: rca camden CAL 156/CDN 1005
1946   cd: cascavelle 210 912

LEO DELIBES (1836-1891)

coppélia, ballet suite
new york   boston
2-4   symphony
december
1953

lp: victor LM 1913/LM 6113
lp: victor (italy) A12R 0131
lp: victor (france) A 630218/43708
lp: hmv ALP 1475
lp: rca camden classics CCV 5030
cd: rca/bmg 09026 619752
excerpts
45: victor ERA 253

sylvia, ballet suite
new york   boston
30-31   symphony
december
1953

lp: victor LM 1913/LM 6113
lp: victor (italy) A12R 0131
lp: victor (france) A 630218/43708
lp: hmv ALP 1475
lp: rca camden classics CCV 5030
cd: rca/bmg 09026 619752
excerpts
45: victor ERA 252

PAUL DUKAS (1865-1935)

l'apprenti sorcier
san francisco 3 february 1952	san francisco symphony	cd: music and arts CD 978
london 1961	london symphony	dvd video: emi 492 8429

ANTONIN DVORAK (1841-1904)

symphony no 7
london
19-20 october 1959

london symphony

lp: victor LM 2489/LSC 2489/RB 16287/ SB 2155/VIC 1310/VICS 1310
lp: london (usa) STS 15157
cd: decca 433 4032

EDWARD ELGAR (1857-1934)

enigma variations
amsterdam
12 october
1950

concertgebouw orchestra

cd: audiophile classics APL 101 560

london
24-25 june
1958

london symphony

lp: victor LM 2418/LSC 2418/RB 16237/ SB 2108/VIC 1107/VICS 1107
lp: london (usa) STS 15188
cd: decca 417 8782/452 3032

MANUEL DE FALLA (1876-1946)

el sombrero de 3 picos, suite
london
15 december
1961

london

cd: bbc classics BBCL 40962

RCA VICTOR

CÉSAR FRANCK
SYMPHONY
IN D MINOR

CHICAGO SYMPHONY
PIERRE MONTEUX

CESAR FRANCK (1822-1890)

symphony in d minor

san francisco 22 april 1941	san francisco symphony	78: victor M 840 78: hmv (france) DB 21442-21446 lp: rca camden CAL 107/CFL 104
san francisco 7 april 1946	san francisco symphony	cd: music and arts CD 978
san francisco 27 february 1950	san francisco symphony	78: victor M 1382 45: victor WDM 1382 lp: victor LM 1065 lp: victor (holland) L 16171 lp: hmv ALP 1019 lp: hmv (france) FALP 123 lp: hmv (germany) WALP 1019
chicago 6 january 1961	chicago symphony	lp: victor LM 2514/LSC 2514 cd: rca/bmg RD 68052/09026 619002/ 09026 619672

les eolides

amsterdam 12 october 1939	concertgebouw orchestra	cd: q-disc Q 97017

franck **piece symphonique in b minor, arranged by o'connell**
san francisco	san francisco	78: victor 18485
22 april	symphony	78: hmv DB 6135/DB 11117
1941		lp: rca camden CAL 215
		cd: rca/bmg 90926 619002/09026 619672
		cd: cascavelle 210 912

psyché et éros/psyché
san francisco	san francisco	cd: music and arts CD 978
3 december	symphony	
1944		

rédemption, symphonic interlude
san francisco	san francisco	cd: music and arts CD 978
13 april	symphony	
1952		

ALEXANDER GLAZUNOV (1865-1936)

scenes de ballet
san francisco	san francisco	cd: music and arts CD 978
12 december	symphony	
1943		

CHRISTOPH WILLIBALD GLUCK (1714-1787)

iphigénie en aulide, overture

san francisco	san francisco	cd: music and arts CD 978
21 january	symphony	
1945		

orfeo ed euridice

rome	rome opera	lp: victor LM 6136/RB 16058-16060
15-26	orchestra	cd: rca/bmg 09026 635342
june	and chorus	*excerpts*
1957	stevens	lp: victor LM 2253/LSC 2253/
	della casa	VIC 1435/VICS 1435
	peters	

dance of the blessed spirits/orfeo ed euridice

london	london	lp: decca LXT 6112/SXL 6112
3-8	symphony	lp: london (usa) CM 9400/CS 6400/
november	c.monteux,	STS 15493
1963	flute	

CHARLES GOUNOD (1818-1893)

faust
new york 19 january 1955	metropolitan opera orchestra and chorus de los angeles miller votipka peerce siepi merrill	lp: melodram MEL 415

faust, ballet music
san francisco 22 december 1947	san francisco symphony	cd: rca/bmg 09026 619752 *unpublished victor 78rpm recording*

la reine de saba, excerpt (plus grand dans son obscurité)
san francisco 19 january 1944	san francisco symphony giannini	cd: eklipse EKRCD 23

LOUIS GRUENBERG (1884-1964)

violin concerto
san francisco 17 december 1945	san francisco symphony heifetz, violin	78: victor M 1079 lp: victor LVT 1017/LCT 1160 lp: victor (france) A 630291 cd: rca/bmg 09026 617542 cd: naxos 811.0942

FRANZ JOSEF HAYDN (1732-1809)

symphony no 88
san francisco	san francisco	cd: music and arts CD 978
21 january	symphony	
1945		

symphony no 94 "surprise"
moscow	boston	lp: melodram MEL 45699
9 september	symphony	
1956		

vienna	vienna	lp: victor LM 2394/LSC 2394/RB 16242/
20-21	philharmonic	SB 2111/220.046
april		lp: decca ECM 574/ECS 574
1959		lp: london (usa) STS 15178
		cd: decca 452 8932

symphony no 101 "clock"
vienna	vienna	lp: victor LM 2394/LSC 2394/RB 16242/
20-21	philharmonic	SB 2111/220.046
april		lp: decca ECM 574/ECS 574
1959		lp: london (usa) STS 15178
		cd: decca 452 8932

PAUL HINDEMITH (1895-1963)

mathis der maler symphony
copenhagen	danish radio	cd: emi CZS 575 4742
11 october	orchestra	
1962		

JOHANN NEPOMUK HUMMEL (1778-1837)

trumpet concerto in f
boston	boston	lp: cambridge CR 1819/CRS 1819
december	chamber	
1963	ensemble	
	ghittala, trumpet	

JACQUES IBERT (1890-1962)

escales
san francisco 2 april 1946	san francisco symphony	78: victor M 1173/V 10 cd: rca/bmg 09026 618952 cd: cascavelle 210 912

VINCENT D'INDY (1851-1931)

symphony no 2
san francisco 2-3 march 1942	san francisco symphony	78: victor M 943 lp: victor LCT 1125 cd: rca/bmg 09026 618882

symphonie cévénole pour piano et orchestre
san francisco 21-22 april 1941	san francisco symphony m.shapiro, piano	78: victor M 913 cd: rca/bmg 09026 618882 cd: cascavelle 210 912

fervaal, prelude
san francisco 27 january 1945	san francisco symphony	78: victor M 1113 lp: rca camden CDN 1005 cd: rca/bmg 09026 618882

istar, symphonic variations
san francisco 27 january 1945	san francisco symphony	78: victor M 1113/SP 16 lp: rca camden CAL 385/CDN 1005 cd: rca/bmg 09026 619002/09026 619672

ARAM KHACHATURIAN (1903-1978)

violin concerto in d minor
boston	boston	lp: victor LM 2220/LSC 2220/
12-13	symphony	VIC 1153/VICS 1153
january	kogan, violin	cd: rca/bmg 09026 637082
1958		

EDOUARD LALO (1823-1892)

symphonie espagnole pour violin et orchestra
san francisco	san francisco	cd: rca/bmg 09026 613952
26-27	symphony	*unpublished victor 78rpm recording*
january	menuhin,	
1945	violin	
san francisco	san francisco	cd: doremi DHR 7736-7737
1950	symphony	*recording incomplete*
	elman, violin	
san francisco	san francisco	cd: music and arts CD 1053
30 december	symphony	
1951	menuhin,	
	violin	

le roi d'ys, overture
san francisco	san francisco	78: victor 11-8489
4 march	symphony	cd: rca/bmg 09026 613952
1942		

FRANZ LISZT (1811-1886)

les préludes

boston	boston	45: victor ERB 5
8 december	symphony	lp: victor LM 1775.LM 6129
1952		lp: victor (france) A 630204
		lp: victor (italy) A12R 0073
		cd: rca/bmg 09026 618902

GUSTAV MAHLER (1860-1911)

kindertotenlieder

san francisco	san francisco	45: victor WDM 1531
26 february	symphony	lp: victor LM 1146
1950	anderson	lp: victor (italy) A12R 0085
		lp: hmv ALP 1138
		cd: rca/bmg 09026 618912

JULES MASSENET (1842-1912)

manon

paris	opéra comique	lp: victor LM 6403
30 may-	orchestra	lp: hmv ALP 1394-1397
7 june	and chorus	lp: capitol GDR 7171
1955	de los angeles	lp: angel ID-6057
	legay	cd: emi CHS 763 5492
	dens	cd: testament SBT 3203
		excerpts
		lp: victor LM 2058
		lp: hmv (france) FALP 165
		recording completed on 22 june 1955

FELIX MENDELSSOHN-BARTHOLDY (1809-1847)

symphony no 4 "italian"
san francisco 23 february 1947	san francisco symphony	cd: music and arts CD 978
manchester 21 november 1962	bbc northern symphony	cd: bbc legends BBCL 40582

the hebrides, overture
san francisco 9 january 1949	san francisco symphony	cd: music and arts CD 978

a midsummer night's dream, suite: overture, scherzo, nocturne and wedding march
vienna 25-28 november 1957	vienna philharmonic	lp: victor LM 2223/LSC 2223/RB 16076/ 　　SB 2014/VIC 1023/VICS 1023 cd: polygram (japan) POCL 4566 *original stereo lp issues omitted the scherzo*

ruy blas, overture
san francisco 22 december 1947	san francisco symphony	78: hmv DB 4323 78: victor 12-0657 45: victor 49-0883
san francisco 27 march 1949	san francisco symphony	cd: music and arts CD 978

OLIVIER MESSIAEN (1908-1992)

3 méditations/l'ascension
san francisco	san francisco	cd: music and arts CD 978
28 march	symphony	cd: cascavelle 210 912
1948		

DARIUS MILHAUD (1892-1974)

protée, second symphonic suite
san francisco	san francisco	78: victor M 1027
14 april	symphony	lp: rca camden CAL 385/CDN 1005
1945		

WOLFGANG AMADEUS MOZART (1756-1791)

symphony no 35 "haffner"

san francisco 24 march 1946	san francisco symphony	cd: music and arts CD 978
hamburg 6-14 february 1964	ndr orchestra	lp: concert hall SMSA 2359 lp: turnabout TV 34831 cd: scribendum SC 013

symphony no 39

hamburg 6-14 february 1964	ndr orchestra	lp: concert hall SMSA 2359 lp: turnabout TV 34831 cd: scribendum SC 013

piano concerto no 12 k414

san francisco 23 april 1950	san francisco symphony kapell, piano	lp: international piano archive IPA 507 cd: music and arts CD 978 *recording may be incomplete*
boston 12 april 1953	boston symphony kraus, piano	lp: victor LM 1783 lp: victor (france) A 630225 lp: victor (italy) A12R 0100 cd: victor (japan) BVCC 37345

piano concerto no 18 k456

boston 13 april 1953	boston symphony kraus, piano	lp: victor LM 1783 lp: victor (france) A 630225 lp: victor (italy) A12R 0100 cd: victor (japan) BVCC 37345

mozart **flute concerto no 2 k314**

london	london	lp: decca LXT 6112/SXL 6112
3-8	symphony	lp: london (usa) CM 9400/CS 6400/
november	c.monteux,	STS 15493
1963	flute	

violin concerto in e k294a

paris	orchestre	78: hmv DB 2268-2270
18 may	symphonique	78: victor M 246
1934	de paris	cd: emi CDH 763 7182
	menuhin,	cd: biddulph LAB 004
	violin	cd: dante LYS 479

don giovanni, overture

san francisco	san francisco	cd: music and arts CD 978
5 february	symphony	
1950		

die entführung aus dem serail, overture

san francisco	san francisco	cd: music and arts CD 978
21 april	symphony	
1945		

idomeneo, overture

amsterdam	concertgebouw	cd: audiophile classics APL 101 592
1956	orchestra	

die zauberflöte, overture

san francisco	san francisco	cd: music and arts CD 978
3 february	symphony	
1952		

MODEST MUSSORGSKY (1839-1881)

night on bare mountain
hamburg	ndr orchestra	lp: concert hall SMSA 2361/SMSA 2548
6-14		lp: turnabout TV 34825
february		cd: scribendum SC 013
1964		

OTTOKAR NOVACEK (1866-1900)

perpetuum mobile, arranged for violin and orchestra
paris	orchestre	78: hmv DB 2283
18 may	symphonique	78: victor M 230
1934	de paris	lp: emi EX 29 08703
	menuhin,	lp: masters of the bow MB 1013
	violin	cd: dante LYS 434-437/LYS 479

JACQUES OFFENBACH (1819-1880)

les contes d'hoffmann
new york	metropolitan	lp: cetra LO 45/DOC 44
3 december	opera orchestra	cd: stradivarius STR 12302
1955	and chorus	
	peters	
	amara	
	stevens	
	tucker	
	singher	
	scott	

NICCOLO PAGANINI (1782-1840)

violin concerto no 1
paris	orchestre	78: hmv DB 2279-2283/DB 8379-8383auto
18 may	symphonique	78: victor M 230
1934	de paris	cd: emi CDH 565 9592
	menuhin,	cd: biddulph LAB 051/LAB 102
	violin	cd: dante LYS 479

WILLEM PIJPER (1894-1947)

symphony no 3
amsterdam	concertgebouw	lp: donemus DCV 9
30 october	orchestra	cd: donemus CVD7-10
1960		

SERGE PROKOFIEV (1891-1953)

symphony no 1 "classical"
paris	orchestre	cd: disques montaigne TCE 8740
8 may	national	
1958		

SERGEI RACHMANINOV (1873-1943)

symphony no 2, second and third movements
san francisco	san francisco	cd: music and arts CD 978
27 february	symphony	
1941		

MAURICE RAVEL (1875-1937)

alborada del gracioso
san francisco	san francisco	78: victor 12-1107
22 december	symphony	cd: rca/bmg 09026 618952
1947		

boléro
wembley	london	lp: philips AL 3500/A02380L/
22-26	symphony	SAL 3500/835 258AY/6527 036/
february		6570 092/6768 339
1964		cd: philips 442 5442/442 5482/
		445 5422/464 7332

daphnis et chloé, complete ballet
amsterdam	concertgebouw	lp: discocorp RR 313
23 june	orchestra	cd: music and arts CD 812
1955	omroepkor	cd: audiophile classics APL 101 549
london	london	lp: decca LXT 5536/SXL 2164
27-28	symphony	lp: london (usa) CM 9028/CS 6147/
april	covent garden	STS 15090
1959	chorus	cd: decca 448 6032

daphnis et chloé, second suite
san francisco	san francisco	78: victor M 1143
3 april	symphony	lp: rca camden CAL 156
1946	university of	cd: rca/bmg 09026 618952
	california	cd: cascavelle 210 912
	chorus	

ravel **ma mere l'oye, complete ballet**
wembley	london	lp: philips AL 3500/A02380L/
22-26	symphony	SAL 3500/835 258AY/6527 038/
february		6570 092/6768 339
1964		cd: philips 442 5442/445 5422/
		464 7332

le petit poucet/ma mere l'oye
paris	orchestre	78: hmv (france) W 1108
3 february	symphonique	cd: dante LYS 374
1930	de paris	cd: cascavelle 210 912

pavane pour une infante défunte
london	london	lp: decca LXT 5677/SXL 2312
11-13	symphony	lp: london (usa) CM 9317/CS 6248/
december		STS 15356
1961		cd: decca 448 6032
		cd: philips 464 7332

rapsodie espagnole
london	london	lp: decca LXT 5677/SXL 2312
11-13	symphony	lp: london (usa) CM 9317/CS 6248/
december		STS 15356
1961		cd: decca 448 6032
		cd: philips 464 7332

ravel **schéhérazade, song cycle**

amsterdam	concertgebouw	cd: music and arts CD 812
20 november	orchestra	cd: audiophile classics APL 101 549
1963	de los angeles	

le tombeau de couperin

new york	new york	cd: new york philharmonic NYP 9708
7 march	philharmonic	
1959		

la valse

paris	orchestre	78: hmv (france) W 1107-1108
31 january	symphonique	cd: dante LYS 374
1930	de paris	cd: cascavelle 210 912

san francisco	san francisco	78: hmv DB 5964-5965
21 april	symphony	78: hmv (australia) ED 316-317
1941		78: victor M 820
		45: rca camden CAE 150
		lp: rca camden CAL 282
		cd: rca/bmg 09026 618952

wembley	london	lp: philips AL 3500/A02380L/
22-26	symphony	SAL 3500/835 258AY/6527 036/
february		6570 092/6580 031/6768 339
1964		cd: philips 442 5442/445 5422/464 7332

valses nobles et sentimentales

san francisco	san francisco	78: hmv DB 6676-6677
3 april	symphony	78: victor M 1143
1946		45: rca camden CAE 216
		lp: rca camden CAL 156
		cd: rca/bmg 09026 618952
		cd: cascavelle 210 912

NIKOLAI RIMSKY-KORSAKOV (1844-1908)

antar, symphonic suite
san francisco 2 april 1946	san francisco symphony	78: hmv DB 6918-6220 78: victor M 1203 cd: rca/bmg 09026 618972

capriccio espagnol
san francisco 13 april 1952	san francisco symphony	cd: music and arts CD 978
hamburg 6-14 february 1964	ndr orchestra	lp: concert hall SMSA 2361 lp: turnabout TV 34668 cd: scribendum SC 013

christmas eve, suite
san francisco 19 december 1943	san francisco symphony	cd: music and arts CD 978

le coq d'or, introduction
san francisco 19 march 1945	san francisco symphony	78: victor M 1252
paris 8 may 1958	orchestre national	cd: disques montaigne TCE 8740

rimsky-korsakov **le coq d'or, cortege**

san francisco 21 april 1941	san francisco symphony	78: hmv DB 5965 78: victor M 820 lp: victor (france) 43361 lp: rca camden CAL 215
paris 8 may 1958	orchestre national	cd: disques montaigne TCE 8740

sadko, suite

san francisco 3 march 1945	san francisco symphony	78: victor M 1252 cd: rca/bmg 09026 618972

scheherazade

san francisco 3-4 march 1942	san francisco symphony	78: victor M 920 45: victor WDM 920/ERC 2 lp: victor LM 1002 lp: victor (italy) A12R 0077 lp: victor (france) 43661 lp: rca camden CAL 451/CDN 1009 cd: rca/bmg 09026 618972
london 7-13 june 1957	london symphony	lp: victor LM 2208/LSC 2208/RB 16077/ SB 2003/VIC 1031/VICS 1031 lp: decca SPA 89 lp: london (usa) STS 15158 cd: london (japan) KICC 8621

tsar sultan, march

san francisco 4 march 1942	san francisco symphony	78: victor M 920 45: victor WDM 920

GIOACCHINO ROSSINI (1792-1868)

il barbiere di siviglia, excerpt (una voce poco fa)
san francisco	san francisco	cd: eklipse EKRCD 55
5 march	symphony	
1950	tourel	

l'italiana in algeri, overture
san francisco	san francisco	cd: music and arts CD 978
6 april	symphony	
1952		

manchester	bbc northern	cd: bbc legends BBCL 40582
21 november	symphony	
1962		

CLAUDE JOSEPH ROUGET DE LISLE (1760-1836)

la marseillaise
walthamstow	london	lp: westminster XWN 2234/WST 234
11-18	symphony	cd: millenium classics MCAD2-9806
june	orchestra	cd: emi CZS 575 4742
1962	and chorus	*rehearsal performance*

CAMILLE SAINT-SAENS (1835-1921)

piano concerto no 4
amsterdam	concertgebouw	cd: q-disc Q 97017
12 october	orchestra	
1939	casadesus, piano	

havanaise pour violon et orchestre
boston	boston	lp: victor LM 2220/LSC 2220/
12-13	symphony	VIC 1153/VICS 1153
january	kogan, violin	
1958		

samson et dalila, excerpt (mon coeur s'ouvre a ta voix)
san francisco	san francisco	cd: eklipse EKRCD 55
18 april	symphony	
1948	tourel	

FRANZ SCHUBERT (1797-1828)

symphony no 8 "unfinished"
amsterdam	concertgebouw	lp: philips A02393L/A02455-02456L/
28-29	orchestra	835 325-835 326AY/6768 339
november		lp: philips classical favourites GL 5788
1963		cd: philips 442 5442

symphony no 9 "great"
moscow	boston	lp: melodiya M10 45701 005
9 september	symphony	
1956		

rosamunde: overture, ballet music no 2 and entr'acte in b flat
vienna	vienna	lp: victor LM 2223/LSC 2223/RB 16076/
25-28	philharmonic	SB 2014/VIC 1023/VICS 1023
november		cd: decca 452 3902
1957		

ständchen, arrangement for soprano and orchestra
san francisco	san francisco	cd: eklipse EKRCD 20
12 december	symphony	
1943	lehmann	

ROBERT SCHUMANN (1810-1856)

symphony no 4
san francisco 7 april 1952	san francisco symphony	45: victor WDM 1714 lp: victor LM 1714
london 18 october 1961	bbc symphony	cd: bbc legends BBCL 40582

piano concerto
new york 13 june 1943	new york philharmonic schnabel, piano	cd: music and arts CD 1111

ALEXANDER SCRIABIN (1872-1915)

poeme de l'extase
san francisco 22 december 1947	san francisco symphony	78: victor M 1270
new york 8 december 1952	boston symphony	lp: victor LM 1775 lp: victor (italy) A12R 0073 lp: victor (france) A 630204 cd: rca/bmg 09026 618902

JEAN SIBELIUS (1865-1957)

symphony no 2
london	london	lp: victor LM 2342/LSC 2342/RB 16186/ SB 2070
18-20	symphony	
june		lp: london (usa) STS 15098
1958		*issued on cd by polygram in japan*

violin concerto
amsterdam	concertgebouw	cd: tahra TAH 175
1 november	orchestra	cd: audiophile classics APL 101.560
1950	damen, violin	

valse triste
san francisco	san francisco	cd: music and arts CD 978
13 march	symphony	
1949		

JOHN PHILIP SOUSA (1854-1932)

stars and stripes forever, march
san francisco	san francisco	cd: music and arts CD 978
7 march	symphony	
1948		

ALESSANDRO STRADELLA (1642-1682)

il floridoro, excerpt (per pieta)
san francisco	san francisco	cd: eklipse EKRCD 55
5 march	symphony	
1950	tourel	

RICHARD STRAUSS (1864-1949)

don juan

san francisco 29 january 1949	san francisco symphony	cd: music and arts CD 978
tanglewood 24 july 1959	boston symphony	cd: music and arts CD 269
manchester 21 december 1960	bbc northern orchestra	cd: bbc legends BBCL 41122

ein heldenleben

san francisco 20 december 1947	san francisco symphony	lp: neiman marcus first edition DMM4-0260 cd: rca/bmg 09026 618892
tanglewood 29 july 1962	boston symphony	cd: music and arts CD 269

strauss **der rosenkavalier, orchestral suite**
san francisco   san francisco   cd: music and arts CD 978
8 october   symphony
1950

till eulenspiegels lustige streiche
san francisco   san francisco   cd: music and arts CD 978
1952   symphony

boston   boston   cd: music and arts CD 269
9 april   symphony
1960

tanglewood   boston   cd: music and arts CD 269
29 july   symphony
1962

tod und verklärung
san francisco   san francisco   cd: music and arts CD 978
13 april   symphony
1952

san francisco   san francisco   lp: victor VIC 1457/VICS 1457
23 january   symphony
1960

IGOR STRAVINSKY (1882-1971)

le sacre du printemps

paris 23-25 january 1929	grand orchestre symphonique	78: hmv (france) W 1016-1019 cd: pearl GEMMCD 9329 cd: dante LYS 374
san francisco 10 march 1945	san francisco symphony	78: hmv DB 6804-6807/DB 9409-9412 auto 78: victor M 1052 lp: rca camden CAL 110
boston 28 january 1951	boston symphony	45: victor WDM 1548 lp: victor LM 1149 lp: victor (italy) A12R 0080 lp: victor (france) 43274 lp: hmv (france) FALP 294 cd: rca/bmg RD 65292/09026 618982
paris 2-11 november 1956	conservatoire orchestra	lp: victor LM 2085/LSC 2085/RB 16007/ SB 2005/VIC 1017/VICS 1017 lp: london (usa) STS 15318 cd: london (japan) KICC 8620
amsterdam 30 october 1960	concertgebouw orchestra	lp: discocorp RR 312

stravinsky **petrouchka**

paris 1928	orchestre symphonique de paris	78: hmv (france) W 1008-1011 cd: pearl GEMMCD 9329
paris 9 june 1955	orchestre national	cd: rappel CD 2
paris 6-10 november 1956	conservatoire orchestra	lp: victor LM 2113/LSC 2113/ RB 16047/SB 2037 cd: decca 452 7222
boston 13 april 1957	boston symphony	lp: discocorp RR 312
paris 8 may 1958	orchestre national	cd: disques montaigne TCE 8740
boston 25-28 january 1959	boston symphony	lp: victor LM 2376/LSC 2376/VICS 1296 lp: rca camden classics CCV 5034
amsterdam 30 october 1960	concertgebouw orchestra	cd: tahra TAH 175

stravinsky **l'oiseau de feu, suite**
paris	conservatoire	lp: victor LM 2113/LSC 2113/RB 16047/
29-30	orchestra	SB 2037/VIC 1027/VICS 1027/
october		VICS 1296
1956		lp: london (usa) STS 15197
		cd: decca 452 7222

symphonie de psaumes
london	bbc symphony	cd: bbc legends BBCL 40962
18 october		
1961		

GIUSEPPE TARTINI (1692-1770)

violin concerto in d minor
san francisco	san francisco	cd: music and arts CD 720
21 january	symphony	
1945	szigeti, violin	

PIOTR TCHAIKOVSKY (1840-1893)

symphony no 4
boston 29 january 1959	boston symphony	lp: victor LM 2369/LSC 2369/RB 16220/ SB 2093/AGL1-5224/GL 11328 lp: victor (france) 43407 cd: rca/bmg 09026 619012

symphony no 5
boston 8 january 1958	boston symphony	lp: victor LM 2239/LM 6902/LSC 2239/ LSC 6902/RB 16161/SB 2045 lp: victor (france) 43407 lp: rca camden classics CCV 5049 cd: rca/bmg 09026 619012
vienna 31 may 1963	london symphony	cd: vanguard classics OVC 8031-8032 *recorded during lso visit to wiener festwochen*
hamburg october 1963	ndr orchestra	lp: concert hall SMSA 2333 cd: priceless D 14155 cd: scribendum SC 013

symphony no 6 "pathétique"

boston
january
1955
	boston
	symphony
		lp: victor LM 1901/LM 6902/LSC 1901/
		    LSC 6902/RB 16143/SB 2024/
		    VIC 1009/VICS 1009
		lp: victor (france) A 630297/43407
		lp: victor (italy) A12R 0173
		lp: hmv ALP 1356
		cd: rca/bmg 09026 619012

tchaikovsky **piano concerto no 1**

london 12-13 june 1957	london symphony entremont, piano	victor/decca unpublished
vienna 31 may 1963	london symphony ogdon, piano	cd: vanguard classics OVC 8031-8032 *recorded during lso visit to wiener festwochen*

romeo and juliet, fantasy overture

san francisco 12 march 1950	san francisco symphony	cd: music and arts CD 978
vienna 31 may 1963	london symphony	cd: vanguard classics OVC 8031-8032 *recorded during lso visit to wiener festwochen*
hamburg 6-14 february 1964	ndr orchestra	lp: concert hall SMSA 2361 cd: scribendum SC 013

tchaikovsky **the sleeping beauty, selection from the ballet**
london	london	lp: victor LM 2177/LM 6097/LSC 2177/
3-6	symphony	LSC 6097/RB 16063/RB 6542/
june		SB 2013/SB 6542/VIC 1011/
1957		VICS 1011
		lp: london (usa) STS 15179
		cd: emi CZS 575 4742

recording completed on 13 june 1957

swan lake, selection from the ballet
walthamstow	london	lp: philips A02261L/835 142AY/
28-29	symphony	6570 187/6768 339
june		cd: philips 420 8722/442 5442/442 5462
1962		*excerpts*
		lp: philips diskothek der meister 610 812VL
		cd: philips 434 5442

the maid of orleans, excerpt (adieu forets)
san francisco	san francisco	cd: eklipse EKRCD 55
18 april	symphony	
1948	tourel	

AMBROISE THOMAS (1811-1896)

mignon, overture
san francisco	san francisco	cd: music and arts CD 978
6 february	symphony	
1949		

GIUSEPPE VERDI (1813-1901)

la traviata
rome	rome opera	lp: victor LM 6040
1-11	orchestra	lp: hmv ALP 1419-1421
june	and chorus	*excerpts*
1956	carteri	lp: victor LM 2044/LM 6061/RB 16089
	valletti	
	warren	

RICHARD WAGNER (1813-1883)

der fliegende holländer, overture
san francisco	san francisco	cd: music and arts CD 978
11 february	symphony	
1951		

paris	orchestre	cd: rappel CD 2
9 june	national	
1955		

hamburg	ndr orchestra	lp: concert hall SMSA 2362
6-14		lp: musidisc FC 435
february		cd: scribendum SC 013
1964		

götterdämmerung, siegfried's rhine journey
san francisco	san francisco	cd: music and arts CD 978
4 march	symphony	
1951		

lohengrin, excerpt (einsam in trüben tagen)
san francisco	san francisco	cd: eklipse EKRCD 56
22 april	symphony	
1950	tourel	

wagner **die meistersinger von nürnberg, overture**

san francisco 16 november 1947	san francisco symphony	cd: music and arts CD 978
london 29 may 1963	london symphony	cd: bbc legends BBCL 40962

die meistersinger von nürnberg, act 3 prelude

chicago 1 january 1961	chicago symphony	cd: chicago symphony orchestra CSOCD 00-06 vhs video: video artists international VAI 69604 dvd video: video artists international VAIDVD 4226

die meistersinger von nürnberg, suite: act 3 prelude; dance of the apprentices; entry of the masters

san francisco 23 april 1950	san francisco symphony	cd: music and arts CD 978

wagner **parsifal, orchestral synthesis from act 3**
san francisco
9 april
1950	san francisco
symphony	cd: music and arts CD 978

rienzi, overture
san francisco
5 february
1950	san francisco
symphony	cd: music and arts CD 978

siegfried, forest murmurs
san francisco
1946-1947	san francisco
symphony	cd: music and arts CD 978

siegfried idyll
san francisco
24 january
1960	san francisco
symphony	lp: victor VIC 1102/VICS 1102/VICS 1457
london
18 november
1960	royal
philharmonic	cd: bbc legends BBCL 40962

tannhäuser, overture and venusberg music
hamburg
6-14
february
1964	ndr orchestra	lp: concert hall SMSA 2362
lp: musidisc FC 435
cd: scribendum SC 013

tristan und isolde, prelude and liebestod
san francisco
6 april
1952	san francisco
symphony	cd: music and arts CD 978
amsterdam
19 february
1953	concertgebouw
orchestra	lp: archive documents AD 103-104
cd: archive documents ADCD 116
cd: king (japan) KICC 2054
all issues of this performance have attributed it to willem mengelberg with incorrect dates 1939-1943
hamburg
6-14
february
1964	ndr orchestra	lp: concert hall SMSA 2362
lp: musidisc FC 435
cd: emi CZS 575 4742
cd: scribendum SC 013

wagner **tristan und isolde, excerpt (mild und leise)**
san francisco   san francisco   lp: discocorp BWS 729
12 december   symphony   cd: eklipse EKRCD 20
1943   lehmann

san francisco   san francisco   cd: eklipse EKRCD 56
22 april   symphony
1950   traubel

die walküre, excerpt (du bist der lenz)
san francisco   san francisco   cd: eklipse EKRCD 56
22 april   symphony
1950   traubel

die walküre, wotan's farewell and magic fire music
san francisco   san francisco   cd: music and arts CD 978
19 january   symphony
1947

CARL MARIA VON WEBER (1786-1826)

konzertstück for piano and orchestra
amsterdam	concertgebouw	cd: audiophile classics APL 101 560
17 october	orchestra	cd: q-disc Q 97017
1939	kraus, piano	

euryanthe, overture
san francisco	san francisco	cd: music and arts CD 978
29 january	symphony	
1950		

MISCELLANEOUS

pierre monteux in interview with roy davies
london   cd: bbc legends BBCL 40582
1961

pierre and doris monteux in interview
toronto   cd: tahra TAH 178
may
1963

Discographies by Travis & Emery:

Discographies by John Hunt.

1987: From Adam to Webern: the Recordings of von Karajan.

1991: 3 Italian Conductors and 7 Viennese Sopranos: 10 Discographies: Arturo Toscanini, Guido Cantelli, Carlo Maria Giulini, Elisabeth Schwarzkopf, Irmgard Seefried, Elisabeth Gruemmer, Sena Jurinac, Hilde Gueden, Lisa Della Casa, Rita Streich.

1992: Mid-Century Conductors and More Viennese Singers: 10 Discographies: Karl Boehm, Victor De Sabata, Hans Knappertsbusch, Tullio Serafin, Clemens Krauss, Anton Dermota, Leonie Rysanek, Eberhard Waechter, Maria Reining, Erich Kunz.

1993: More 20th Century Conductors: 7 Discographies: Eugen Jochum, Ferenc Fricsay, Carl Schuricht, Felix Weingartner, Josef Krips, Otto Klemperer, Erich Kleiber.

1994: Giants of the Keyboard: 6 Discographies: Wilhelm Kempff, Walter Gieseking, Edwin Fischer, Clara Haskil, Wilhelm Backhaus, Artur Schnabel.

1994: Six Wagnerian Sopranos: 6 Discographies: Frieda Leider, Kirsten Flagstad, Astrid Varnay, Martha Moedl, Birgit Nilsson, Gwyneth Jones.

1995: Musical Knights: 6 Discographies: Henry Wood, Thomas Beecham, Adrian Boult, John Barbirolli, Reginald Goodall, Malcolm Sargent.

1995: A Notable Quartet: 4 Discographies: Gundula Janowitz, Christa Ludwig, Nicolai Gedda, Dietrich Fischer-Dieskau.

1996: The Post-War German Tradition: 5 Discographies: Rudolf Kempe, Joseph Keilberth, Wolfgang Sawallisch, Rafael Kubelik, Andre Cluytens.

1996: Teachers and Pupils: 7 Discographies: Elisabeth Schwarzkopf, Maria Ivoguen, Maria Cebotari, Meta Seinemeyer, Ljuba Welitsch, Rita Streich, Erna Berger.

1996: Tenors in a Lyric Tradition: 3 Discographies: Peter Anders, Walther Ludwig, Fritz Wunderlich.

1997: The Lyric Baritone: 5 Discographies: Hans Reinmar, Gerhard Hüsch, Josef Metternich, Hermann Uhde, Eberhard Wächter.

1997: Hungarians in Exile: 3 Discographies: Fritz Reiner, Antal Dorati, George Szell.

1997: The Art of the Diva: 3 Discographies: Claudia Muzio, Maria Callas, Magda Olivero.

1997: Metropolitan Sopranos: 4 Discographies: Rosa Ponselle, Eleanor Steber, Zinka Milanov, Leontyne Price.

1997: Back From The Shadows: 4 Discographies: Willem Mengelberg, Dimitri Mitropoulos, Hermann Abendroth, Eduard Van Beinum.

1997: More Musical Knights: 4 Discographies: Hamilton Harty, Charles Mackerras, Simon Rattle, John Pritchard.

1998: Conductors On The Yellow Label: 8 Discographies: Fritz Lehmann, Ferdinand Leitner, Ferenc Fricsay, Eugen Jochum, Leopold Ludwig, Artur Rother, Franz Konwitschny, Igor Markevitch.

1998: More Giants of the Keyboard: 5 Discographies: Claudio Arrau, Gyorgy Cziffra, Vladimir Horowitz, Dinu Lipatti, Artur Rubinstein.

1998: Mezzos and Contraltos: 5 Discographies: Janet Baker, Margarete Klose, Kathleen Ferrier, Giulietta Simionato, Elisabeth Höngen.
1999: The Furtwängler Sound Sixth Edition: Discography and Concert Listing.
1999: The Great Dictators: 3 Discographies: Evgeny Mravinsky, Artur Rodzinski, Sergiu Celibidache.
1999: Sviatoslav Richter: Pianist of the Century: Discography.
2000: Philharmonic Autocrat 1: Discography of: Herbert Von Karajan [Third Edition].
2000: Wiener Philharmoniker 1 - Vienna Philharmonic & Vienna State Opera Orchestras: Disc. Part 1 1905-1954.
2000: Wiener Philharmoniker 2 - Vienna Philharmonic & Vienna State Opera Orchestras: Disc. Part 2 1954-1989.
2001: Gramophone Stalwarts: 3 Separate Discographies: Bruno Walter, Erich Leinsdorf, Georg Solti.
2001: Singers of the Third Reich: 5 Discographies: Helge Roswaenge, Tiana Lemnitz, Franz Völker, Maria Müller, Max Lorenz.
2001: Philharmonic Autocrat 2: Concert Register of Herbert Von Karajan Second Edition.
2002: Sächsische Staatskapelle Dresden: Complete Discography.
2002: Carlo Maria Giulini: Discography and Concert Register.
2002: Pianists For The Connoisseur: 6 Discographies: Arturo Benedetti Michelangeli, Alfred Cortot, Alexis Weissenberg, Clifford Curzon, Solomon, Elly Ney.
2003: Singers on the Yellow Label: 7 Discographies: Maria Stader, Elfriede Trötschel, Annelies Kupper, Wolfgang Windgassen, Ernst Häfliger, Josef Greindl, Kim Borg.
2003: A Gallic Trio: 3 Discographies: Charles Münch, Paul Paray, Pierre Monteux.
2004: Antal Dorati 1906-1988: Discography and Concert Register.
2004: Columbia 33CX Label Discography.
2004: Great Violinists: 3 Discographies: David Oistrakh, Wolfgang Schneiderhan, Arthur Grumiaux.
2006: Leopold Stokowski: Second Edition of the Discography.
2006: Wagner Im Festspielhaus: Discography of the Bayreuth Festival.
2006: Her Master's Voice: Concert Register and Discography of Dame Elisabeth Schwarzkopf [Third Edition].
2007: Hans Knappertsbusch: Kna: Concert Register and Discography of Hans Knappertsbusch, 1888-1965. Second Edition.
2008: Philips Minigroove: Second Extended Version of the European Discography.
2009: American Classics: The Discographies of Leonard Bernstein and Eugene Ormandy.

Discography by Stephen J. Pettitt, edited by John Hunt:
1987: Philharmonia Orchestra: Complete Discography 1945-1987

Available from: Travis & Emery at 17 Cecil Court, London, UK. (+44) 20 7 240 2129. email on sales@travis-and-emery.com .

© Travis & Emery 2009

Music and Books published by Travis & Emery Music Bookshop:

Anon.: Hymnarium Sarisburense, cum Rubris et Notis Musicus
Agricola, Johann Friedrich from Tosi: Anleitung zur Singkunst. (Faksimile 1757)
Bach, C.P.E.: edited W. Emery: Nekrolog or Obituary Notice of J.S. Bach.
Bateson, Naomi Judith: Alcock of Salisbury
Bathe, William: A Briefe Introduction to the Skill of Song
Bax, Arnold: Symphony #5, Arranged for Piano Four Hands by Walter Emery
Burney, Charles: The Present State of Music in France and Italy
Burney, Charles: The Present State of Music in Germany, The Netherlands …
Burney, Charles: An Account of the Musical Performances … Handel
Burney, Karl: Nachricht von Georg Friedrich Handel's Lebensumstanden.
Burns, Robert (jnr): The Caledonian Musical Museum (1810 volume)
Cobbett, W.W.: Cobbett's Cyclopedic Survey of Chamber Music. (2 vols.)
Corrette, Michel: Le Maitre de Clavecin
Crimp, Bryan: Dear Mr. Rosenthal … Dear Mr. Gaisberg …
Crimp, Bryan: Solo: The Biography of Solomon
d'Indy, Vincent: Beethoven: Biographie Critique
d'Indy, Vincent: Beethoven: A Critical Biography
d'Indy, Vincent: César Franck (in French)
Fischhof, Joseph: Versuch einer Geschichte des Clavierbaues
Frescobaldi, Girolamo: D'Arie Musicali per Cantarsi. Primo Libro & Secondo Libro.
Geminiani, Francesco: The Art of Playing the Violin.
Handel; Purcell; Boyce; Green et al: Calliope or English Harmony: Volume First.
Hawkins, John: A General History of the Science and Practice of Music (5 vols.)
Herbert-Caesari, Edgar: The Science and Sensations of Vocal Tone
Herbert-Caesari, Edgar: Vocal Truth
Hopkins and Rimboult: The Organ. Its History and Construction.
Hunt, John: some 40 discographies – see list of discographies
Isaacs, Lewis: Hänsel and Gretel. A Guide to Humperdinck's Opera.
Isaacs, Lewis: Königskinder (Royal Children) A Guide to Humperdinck's Opera.
Lacassagne, M. l'Abbé Joseph : Traité Général des élémens du Chant.
Lascelles (née Catley), Anne: The Life of Miss Anne Catley.
Mainwaring, John: Memoirs of the Life of the Late George Frederic Handel
Malcolm, Alexander: A Treaty of Music: Speculative, Practical and Historical
Marx, Adolph Bernhard: Die Kunst des Gesanges, Theoretisch-Practisch
May, Florence: The Life of Brahms
Mellers, Wilfrid: Angels of the Night: Popular Female Singers of Our Time
Mellers, Wilfrid: Bach and the Dance of God

Travis & Emery Music Bookshop
17 Cecil Court, London, WC2N 4EZ, United Kingdom.
Tel. (+44) 20 7240 2129

Music and Books published by Travis & Emery Music Bookshop:

Mellers, Wilfrid: Beethoven and the Voice of God
Mellers, Wilfrid: Caliban Reborn - Renewal in Twentieth Century Music
Mellers, Wilfrid: François Couperin and the French Classical Tradition
Mellers, Wilfrid: Harmonious Meeting
Mellers, Wilfrid: Le Jardin Retrouvé, The Music of Frederic Mompou
Mellers, Wilfrid: Music and Society, England and the European Tradition
Mellers, Wilfrid: Music in a New Found Land: … … American Music
Mellers, Wilfrid: Romanticism and the Twentieth Century (from 1800)
Mellers, Wilfrid: The Masks of Orpheus: …… the Story of European Music.
Mellers, Wilfrid: The Sonata Principle (from c. 1750)
Mellers, Wilfrid: Vaughan Williams and the Vision of Albion
Panchianio, Cattuffio: Rutzvanscad Il Giovine.
Pearce, Charles: Sims Reeves, Fifty Years of Music in England.
Pettitt, Stephen: Philharmonia Orchestra: Complete Discography 1945-1987
Playford, John: An Introduction to the Skill of Musick.
Purcell, Henry et al: Harmonia Sacra … The First Book, (1726)
Purcell, Henry et al: Harmonia Sacra … Book II (1726)
Quantz, Johann: Versuch einer Anweisung die Flöte traversiere zu spielen.
Rameau, Jean-Philippe: Code de Musique Pratique, ou Methodes.
Rastall, Richard: The Notation of Western Music.
Rimbault, Edward: The Pianoforte, Its Origins, Progress, and Construction.
Rousseau, Jean Jacques: Dictionnaire de Musique
Rubinstein, Anton : Guide to the proper use of the Pianoforte Pedals.
Sainsbury, John S.: Dictionary of Musicians. Vol. 1. (1825). 2 vols.
Simpson, Christopher: A Compendium of Practical Musick in Five Parts
Spohr, Louis: Autobiography
Spohr, Louis: Grand Violin School
Tans'ur, William: A New Musical Grammar; or The Harmonical Spectator
Terry, Charles Sanford: Four-Part Chorals of J.S. Bach. (German & English)
Terry, Charles Sanford: Joh. Seb. Bach, Cantata Texts, Sacred and Secular.
Terry, Charles Sanford: The Origins of the Family of Bach Musicians.
Tosi, Pierfrancesco: Opinioni de' Cantori Antichi, e Moderni
Van der Straeten, Edmund: History of the Violoncello, The Viol da Gamba …
Van der Straeten, Edmund: History of the Violin, Its Ancestors… (2 vols.)
Walther, J. G.: Musicalisches Lexikon ober Musicalische Bibliothec (1732)

Travis & Emery Music Bookshop
17 Cecil Court, London, WC2N 4EZ, United Kingdom.
Tel. (+44) 20 7240 2129

© Travis & Emery 2009

www.ingramcontent.com/pod-product-compliance
Lightning Source LLC
Chambersburg PA
CBHW071841230426
43671CB00012B/2028